Reach Out

Student Book 2

Ben Wetz

James Styring • Nicholas Tims

OXFORD

UNIVERSITY PRESS

 CONTENTS

Starter unit

1 🔘 1.02 **Check the meaning of words 1–14. Then match words 1–8 with the words in the box. Listen and check.**

> brother ~~father~~ grandfather grandson
> husband nephew son uncle

1 mother **father**	8 niece
2 sister	9 cousin
3 aunt	10 child
4 grandmother	11 parent
5 wife	12 grandparent
6 daughter	13 partner
7 granddaughter	14 twin

2 **Look at the pictures and choose the correct words.**

This is Brad Pitt and (partner) / brother Angelina Jolie with their ¹**nieces / children**. Their three ²**twins / sons** are Maddox, Pax, and Knox. Their ³**daughters / cousins** are Zahara, Shiloh, and Vivienne.

William and Harry are ⁴**brothers / cousins**. Their ⁵**grandmother / aunt** is the Queen of England.

3 **Choose the odd word out in each group.**

1 father   uncle   grandmother   grandson
2 nephew   wife   sister   aunt
3 husband   mother   father   daughter

4 **ACTIVATE** Work in pairs. Ask and answer questions about your families using the key phrases.

> **KEY PHRASES** ⭕ **Asking about families**
>
> Do you have any brothers and sisters?
> What's your father's name?
> Do you have a favorite uncle or aunt?
> Where's your mother from?
> How old is your grandfather?

> Do you have any brothers?   Yes, I do.

Bart Simpson has two ⁶**sisters / fathers**, Lisa and Maggie. Marge is their ⁷**daughter / mother**, and her ⁸**husband's / wife's** name is Homer.

LANGUAGE FOCUS ● *be* + subject pronouns • Possessive *'s*
I can exchange personal information.

be + subject pronouns

1 Complete the table using the correct form of *be*.

Affirmative
She's happy today.

Negative
She ¹___ happy today.

Question
² ___ she happy today?

2 Complete the sentences using the affirmative form of *be*. Then write the negative and question forms.

1 You ___ in my class.
2 It ___ a nice day.
3 I ___ fourteen years old.
4 Your cousins ___ in California.
5 We ___ partners.

(More practice ⇨ Workbook page 5)

3 Complete the sentences using the correct form of *be* and subject pronouns.

Paul and Lily aren't here. **They're** in a different class.
1 No, ___ sixteen. I'm fourteen.
2 ___ your sister? No, she isn't.
3 What time ___ ? It's five past three.
4 This is my uncle. ___ a teacher.
5 ___ from Dallas? Yes, they are.
6 My parents are happy with my brother and me because ___ good at school.

4 Write questions using *be* and the words in the boxes. Then ask and answer with a partner.

> you   your teacher   your grandparents
> your best friend   your mother or father

> from here?   strict?   good at English?
> nice?   interested in music?
> in this class?   (a) soccer fan(s)?

> *Is your teacher from here?*   *Yes, he is.*

Possessive *'s*

5 Translate the sentences. When do we use *'s* and when do we use the apostrophe (')?

1 My cousins' house is very big.
2 Ethan's father is in Canada.
3 Where are Ryan and Amy's books?

(More practice ⇨ Workbook page 5)

6 Write sentences using possessive *'s*.

This is (my uncle / car).
This is my uncle's car.
1 I like (Keira / hair).
2 Is that (David and Julie / mother)?
3 It's my (grandmother / birthday).
4 My (parents / car) isn't here.
5 What are (your friends / names)?

7 **ACTIVATE** Find out more about people in your class. Match 1–8 with a–h to make questions. Then ask and answer the questions.

1 How old ...   a your parents' names?
2 Where ...   b are you?
3 Who's your ...   c you today?
4 When's ...   d the next class?
5 What time's ...   e phone number?
6 What are ...   f favorite singer?
7 How are ...   g your birthday?
8 What's your ...   h are you from?

> *How old are you?*   *I'm fourteen.*

> ○ *Finished?*
> **Write a short paragraph about you.**
> *My name's Jacob and I'm fourteen years old ...*

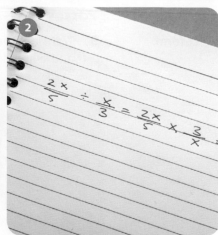

1 Write combinations of nouns for pictures 1–6 using the words in the box. You can use the words more than once.

> geography class science test math
> book computer science teacher French
> homework history notes music
> exercise English laboratory P.E.* room

*P.E. = Physical Education

1 science laboratory

2 Choose the correct words.

1 This geography **exercise / laboratory** is easy.
2 I have a list of verbs in my **English / history** notes.
3 She's in the music **exercise / room**.
4 I don't have my math **homework / room**.
5 We have a big gymnasium for **P.E. / geography** classes.
6 My French **teacher / test** has a good accent.
7 It's on page twelve of your science **exercise / book**.

3 ACTIVATE Study the key phrases. Then ask and answer questions about schoolwork with a partner. Change the words in blue.

> **KEY PHRASES ◯ Talking about schoolwork**
>
> Do we have math homework today?
> When's the geography test?
> Can I look at your history notes?
> Who's your computer science teacher?
> What time's the next English class?

> Do we have science homework today?

> Yes, we do.

LANGUAGE FOCUS ■ *have* • *there is, there are*
I can talk about school.

have

1 Complete the tables using the correct form of *have*.

Affirmative	
I / You have He / She / It has We / They ¹ ___	geography today. a strict teacher. Spanish homework.

Negative	
I / You don't have He / She / It ² ___ have We / They ³ ___ have	geography today. a strict teacher. Spanish homework.

Questions	
Do I / you have Does he / she / it have Do we / they ⁴ ___	geography today? a strict teacher? Spanish homework?

More practice ⇨ Workbook page 7

2 Order the words to make sentences.

have / a / math book / good / we / don't
We don't have a good math book.
1 my sister / classes / history / have / doesn't
2 our / books / the teacher / does / have / ?
3 what / for / have / we / do / exercises / homework / ?
4 has / our school / a good science laboratory
5 computer science / notes / I / have / don't / your

3 Write eight questions using *have* and the words in boxes A–C. Then ask and answer with a partner.

A you   our school   your friends
your teacher   this English book

B good   interesting   strict   difficult
neat   nice

C classes?   writing?   teachers?   notes?
exercises?   topics?   rooms?

Do you have neat writing?   *Yes, I do.*

there is, there are

4 Complete the table with the words in the box. There are two words that you do not need. When do we use *any*?

are   are   is   is   isn't   's

Affirmative	
Singular	There's a test on Friday.
Plural	There ¹ ___ three people here.

Negative	
Singular	There ² ___ a test on Friday.
Plural	There aren't any people here.

Questions	
Singular	³ ___ there a test on Friday?
Plural	Are there any people here?

More practice ⇨ Workbook page 7

5 Complete the sentences using the correct form of *there is* and *there are*.

1 ___ a teacher in the geography class?
2 No, ___ any teachers.
3 ___ two new people in this class.
4 ___ any math homework today?
5 ___ a science laboratory next to this room.
6 No, ___ a music room in my school. We don't study music.
7 Yes, ___ three exercises for homework.
8 ___ any notes in your book?

6 ACTIVATE Complete the questions using the correct forms of *be* and *have*. Then talk about school with a partner.

1 ___ there an English test this week?
2 Do you ___ a new teacher for science?
3 What time ___ the next class?
4 ___ the English teacher from Australia?
5 ___ there any new students in this class?
6 When ___ our next math class?
7 What teacher do we ___ for computer science this year?

Is there an English test this week?

No, there isn't.

1

Possessions

Start thinking

1 What are your favorite possessions?
2 What is a monastery? Who lives there?
3 What do you do in your free time?

Aims

Communication: I can ...

- talk about my possessions.
- talk about school rules.
- talk about habits and facts.
- talk about my free time.
- ask and answer about free-time activities.
- ask for and give opinions.
- write about my likes and dislikes.

Vocabulary

- Everyday objects
- Free-time activities

Language focus

- Simple present: affirmative and negative
- Adverbs of frequency
- Simple present: questions
- Capital letters and punctuation

Reach Out Options

Extra listening and speaking

Joining a club

⟹ Page 88

Curriculum extra

Technology: Advertising

⟹ Page 96

Culture

Allowance

⟹ Page 104

Vocabulary puzzles

Everyday objects;
Free-time activities

⟹ Page 112

VOCABULARY ◼ Everyday objects

I can talk about my possessions.

1 🔘 1.03 Match the words in the box with objects a–j on page 9. Then listen and check.

> backpack   bus pass   clothes   ID card   keys
> cell phone   money   MP3 player   tickets   wallet

2 Check the meaning of the words in the box. Then complete the sentences with the words.

> jewelry   key ring   laptop   makeup   purse
> sunglasses   watch

1 "Do you have a computer at home?" "Yes, I use my dad's ___."
2 "What time is it?" "I don't know. I don't have a ___."
3 My sister keeps her money in her ___.
4 I can't find my keys. They're on a blue ___.
5 It's sunny today. I'm going to wear ___.
6 I have some gold and silver ___, but I don't wear it to school.
7 My grandma has a pretty face and she doesn't wear ___.

3 Look at the questionnaire on page 9. Check the meaning of the six adjectives in blue in the key.

4 Do the questionnaire with a partner. Then look at the key. Do you agree with the results?

5 Write five sentences about your answers to the questionnaire.

I have an old cell phone. I'm not very trendy!

6 **ACTIVATE** Work in pairs. Ask and answer questions about your possessions.

> Do you have a bus pass?

> Yes, I do. / No, I don't.

⭕ *Finished?*
Look again at the questionnaire on page 9. Write five sentences about a friend or someone in your family.
My sister: She's sentimental. She keeps pictures of her friends, especially her boyfriend ...

Your things, your character

What do your possessions say about you?

1 Do you get a new cell phone every year?

a No, I don't need a new cell phone. Old phones send the same texts!
b No. I like the new phones but they're too expensive. I have an old one.
c Yes! The newest cell phones are cool.

2 Do you have a collection of ticket stubs and bus passes at home?

a Yes, I have a big box. I collect everything.
b Some. I only keep tickets from my favorite movies.
c No! I don't collect things.

3 Do you have pictures on your cell phone or in your wallet?

a Yes, lots.
b Just one or two.
c No, none.

4 Are all your clothes new?

a No, old clothes are more comfortable.
b They're not all new. I wear old clothes at home and new clothes to go out.
c Yes! I love new clothes. Fashion is my life.

5 Do you have your MP3 player here now?

a Yes. It's always in my pocket.
b Usually, but today I forgot it.
c No. I can never find it.

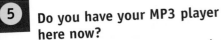

6 Do you always have your keys and money with you?

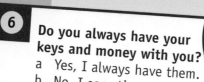
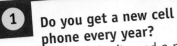

a Yes, I always have them.
b No, I sometimes lose my keys.
c Never. I always forget something!

7 Do you always have your ID card with you?

a Yes, of course. It's important and I need it.
b No, I sometimes leave it at home.
c Never. I lose one every week!

8 What is in your backpack today?

a I always have the same possessions with me.
b I'm not sure, but there's usually a surprise!
c I don't know. I can't remember everything!

KEY

Questions 1–4

Mostly a: You're sentimental. You love your memories and old possessions.
Mostly b: You're sensible. You remember the past, but you think about the future too.
Mostly c: You're trendy. You only think about the future. The past is just a memory.

Questions 5–8

Mostly a: You're very organized. You know where all your possessions are.
Mostly b: You know where most of your possessions are, but not all the time!
Mostly c: You're disorganized. You must be more careful with your possessions.

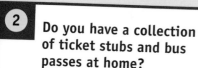
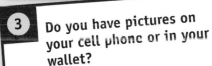

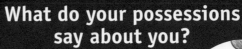

I don't go out without …

I'm a monk and a monk doesn't go out without his robes!

In Thailand, most Buddhist schoolboys become monks for a year. A monk lives with almost no possessions.
A monk lives in a monastery and he is supposed to wear orange robes.
A monk doesn't wear jeans or T-shirts.

It's against the rules to have jewelry and cell phones in the monastery, but we are allowed to have some family pictures. My only other possessions are a bowl, a cup, sandals, and an umbrella. Every day, very early in the morning, we walk around the streets with our bowls and people give us food. Why? We aren't supposed to have money, so we can't buy food.

Phra Pachak, 13, Chiang Mai, Thailand

Natalie, 14, Georgia, U.S.

I don't go out without my polo shirt and my purse. The polo shirt is part of our school uniform. I have a house key, my library card, and my electronic ID card in my purse. School's OK, but it's very strict. We use the ID card when we arrive at school and when we go into each class. The principal doesn't ask the teachers how many classes we go to. The ID card gives the principal this information!

We use the ID cards to pay for lunch, so we don't use money at school. I have a cell phone, but we aren't allowed to use our phones at school. It's against the rules.

1 Check the meaning of words 1–5. Then look at the photos. Which possessions do you think are Phra Pachak's and which are Natalie's?

1 bowl   3 sandals   5 umbrella
2 library card   4 polo shirt

2 Read the study strategy. Then use the strategy to check your answers in exercise 1.

STUDY STRATEGY ○ Scanning

To find answers in a text quickly, "scan" the text:
1 Identify the key word(s) in the question.
2 Read the text quickly. Don't stop at difficult words. Only stop at the key words.
3 Read that part of the text again and check.

3   🔊 1.04   Listen and read the texts. Then write *true* or *false*. Correct the false sentences.

1 Thai monks wear orange T-shirts.
2 Monks don't talk to their families on cell phones.
3 People give money to the monks.
4 All the students at Natalie's school wear a polo shirt.
5 Natalie doesn't go to class without a library card.
6 Natalie uses an ID card instead of money.

4 **BUILD YOUR VOCABULARY** Complete the sentences with the words in the text in blue.

He **is supposed to** wear orange robes.
1 We __ __ __ have money.
2 __ __ __ __ __ have jewelry.
3 We __ __ __ have some family pictures.
4 We __ __ __ use our phones at school.

5 **ABOUT YOU** Ask and answer the questions.

1 Are you allowed to take cell phones to school?
2 Are you allowed to wear jewelry at school?
3 What are you supposed to do when you arrive every morning?
4 What is against the rules at your school?

> We're allowed to take cell phones to school.

> Yes, but we aren't supposed to use them in class.

LANGUAGE FOCUS ● Simple present: affirmative and negative
I can talk about habits and facts.

1

1 Complete the sentences with the words in the box. Check your answers in the texts on page 10.

> don't   don't   ~~doesn't~~   doesn't   give
> lives   walk

A monk **doesn't** go out without his robes.
1 A monk ___ in a monastery.
2 A monk ___ wear jeans or T-shirts.
3 We ___ around the streets.
4 People ___ us food.
5 I ___ go out without my polo shirt on.
6 We ___ use money at school.

2 Complete the rules with the words in the box.

> don't   doesn't   facts   routines

⭕ **RULES**

1 We use the simple present to talk about habits, ___, and ___.
2 We use ___ + base form of the verb after *I / you / we/ they*.
3 We use ___ + base form of the verb after *he / she / it*.

(More practice ⇨ Workbook page 9)

3 Write true sentences. Use affirmative or negative forms of the verbs.

we / need / ID cards   **We don't need ID cards.**
1 I / like / jewelry
2 my parents / use / a laptop
3 I / collect / movie ticket stubs
4 we / wear / jeans at school
5 our teachers / give / us lots of homework
6 I / study / Spanish
7 my best friends / live / near me
8 we / start / school at 8:30 a.m.

4 Study the spelling rules. Then complete the table using the words in the box.

> ~~carry~~   copy   finish   go   live   mix
> ~~need~~   pass   study   try   use   walk
> watch   wear

Spelling rules: third person (*he / she / it*)		
Most verbs: add -s	Verbs ending in consonant + -y: -y → add -ies	Verbs ending in -o, -ch, -sh, -x, -ss: add -es
needs	*carries*	

(Pronunciation: Third person singular ⇨ Workbook page 90)

5 Complete the text using the affirmative or negative form of the verbs in parentheses.

Ali Ahmadi, 15, *lives* (live) in Iran. Ali and his family are nomads, and they ¹___ (live) in tents. Ali's father ²___ (keep) camels and goats. Ali ³___ (not go) to school, so his mother ⁴___ (help) Ali to read and write. Ali ⁵___ (speak) Farsi, the national Iranian language, and Bakhtiari, a nomadic language. The nomads ⁶___ (not use) MP3 players and ID cards. They ⁷___ (prefer) a simple life.

6 **ACTIVATE** Make four affirmative and four negative true sentences using the words in the box. Then compare with a partner.

> a laptop   a new phone   an MP3 player
> carry   English   live   lots of money
> need   new clothes   speak   study
> sunglasses   use   want   wear

You use a laptop. I don't use a laptop.

⭕ *Finished?*
Write a message to Ali Ahmadi. Tell him about your life and your possessions.
Hi Ali, my name's Zelda. I'm 14 and I live in...

1 ⏺ **1.05** Choose the correct words. Then listen and check.

1 watch **magazines / TV**
2 listen to **music / the movies**
3 play **the Internet / computer games**
4 meet **things / friends**
5 play **sports / bike riding**
6 collect **things / Spanish**
7 take **MP3s / pictures**
8 go **shopping / shopping mall**
9 surf **TV / the Internet**
10 go **swimming / soccer**
11 play **singing / in a band**
12 go **tennis / bike riding**
13 go **to the movies / movie**
14 read **magazines and books / money**

2 ⏺ **1.06** Read the information about the *Money Matters* podcast. Then listen and choose the correct answers.

1 Justine goes metal detecting with ...
   a her friends.   b her dad.   c her mom.
2 Justine goes metal detecting ...
   a on the weekends.
   b when she is on vacation.
   c after school.
3 Justine usually goes metal detecting ...
   a near the ocean.   c in the park.
   b at school.
4 Justine ...
   a has $183 from metal detecting.
   b pays $183 a year to go metal detecting.
   c bought her metal detector for $183.

Language point: Adverbs of frequency

3 ⏺ **1.06** Study the diagram. Then order sentences a–f. Start with the least frequent. What is the position of the adverbs with *be*, *have*, and other verbs?

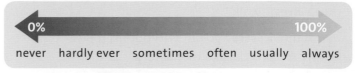

0%   100%

never   hardly ever   sometimes   often   usually   always

(More practice ⇨ Workbook page 11)

___ a You hardly ever find a hobby that pays you.
___ b It's usually me and my dad.
___ c I always have free time then.
___ d We sometimes go to the beach.
 1 e We never find gold.
___ f We often find modern coins.

4 Write true sentences using the simple present and adverbs of frequency.

I / meet / my friends after school
I often meet my friends after school.

1 we / play / computer games
2 I / go / swimming
3 my friends and I / watch / DVDs
4 I / have / a cell phone with me
5 I / be / late for class
6 my friends and I / go / bike riding

5 ACTIVATE Work in pairs. Talk about your free time. Use the simple present and adverbs of frequency.

(*I always go shopping on Saturdays. I love it!*)

(*I'm always busy on Saturdays, so I don't go shopping. I usually play soccer.*)

Hobbies that pay

Some hobbies are free. Others are expensive! But Justine Meyer **makes** money from her hobby! Listen to her story.

▼ Podcast

LANGUAGE FOCUS ◼ Simple present: questions
I can ask and answer about free-time activities.

1 🔊 1.07 Complete the mini-dialogues with *do, don't, does,* or *doesn't*. Then listen and check.

> **Do** you listen to music at home?

> Yes, I **do**. / No, I **don't**.

> ¹___ he play in a band?

> Yes, he ²___. / No, he ³___!

> ⁴___ they play sports?

> Yes, they ⁵___. / No, they ⁶___!

> More practice ⟹ Workbook page 11

2 Complete the questions using the simple present form of the verbs in parentheses.

Does your best friend **collect** things? (collect)
1 ___ you ___ the Internet? (surf)
2 ___ your friend ___ bike riding? (go)
3 ___ your friends ___ computer games? (play)
4 ___ your friend ___ a cell phone? (use)
5 ___ you ___ to classical music? (listen)
6 ___ your parents ___ lots of pictures? (take)

3 Work in pairs. Ask and answer the questions in exercise 2. Use short answers.

> Does your best friend collect things?

> Yes, he does. He collects shoes!

4 🔊 1.08 Read the answers and complete the questions with the words in the box. Then listen and check.

> ~~What~~ When Where Who Why

What do you need?
You need a metal detector.
1 ___ do you go?
Over my summer vacation.
2 ___ does she go over her vacation?
Because she always has free time then.
3 ___ do they go?
They usually go to a park.
4 ___ do you usually go with?
I go with my dad.

> More practice ⟹ Workbook page 11

5 Write questions for the answers using *what, when, where, who,* and *why*.

you / meet / your friends after school
Why do you meet your friends after school?
Because we go to the park.
1 you / read / in your free time
I read magazines.
2 you / study / English
Because I want to pass my tests.
3 you and your friends / play / sports
We play sports on Friday afternoons.
4 you / do / on the weekend
We go shopping on the weekend.
5 your best friend / meet / you
He meets me in the park.
6 go to the movies / with
I go to the movies with my best friend.

6 ACTIVATE Work in pairs. Ask and answer the questions in exercise 5. Use true answers.

> Why do you meet your friends after school?

> Because we often play sports.

> ⃝ *Finished?*
> **Write six more interview questions for a friend.**
> 1 Do you play any sports?
> 2 When do you play?
> 3 …

Leah	Hey, Shaun, look at this.
Shaun	What?
Leah	This hat! What do you think?
Shaun	It's not great.
Leah	It's very trendy.
Shaun	Well, I can't ¹___ it!
Leah	Oh, well, we can't all have good taste!
Shaun	What about this T-shirt?
Leah	It's OK, ²___.
Shaun	Don't ³___? I think ⁴___.
Leah	No, I'm not ⁵___ red.
Shaun	Well, it's better than my brown and blue shirt!
Leah	Ha! That's true.

5 Invent mini-dialogues about possessions 1–6. Use the words in the box and your own ideas.

> cool   pretty   trendy   unusual   useful

Do you like this bag?

Yes, I do. I think it's really cool.

1 Look at the picture of Shaun and Leah. Where are they?

2  1.09 Listen to the dialogue. What do Shaun and Leah think of the clothes?

3 Study the key phrases. Are responses a–e positive or negative?

KEY PHRASES ○ Asking for and giving opinions

What do you think?
Don't you like it?
a It's OK, I suppose. positive
b I can't stand … .
c It's not great.
d I'm not crazy about … .
e I think it's really nice.

4 1.09 Complete the dialogue with the key phrases. Then listen again and check. Now practice the dialogue with a partner.

6 **ACTIVATE** Work in pairs. Imagine you want to buy one or two of the things in exercise 5. Invent a dialogue with your partner. Use the dialogue in exercise 4 as a model and change the words in blue.

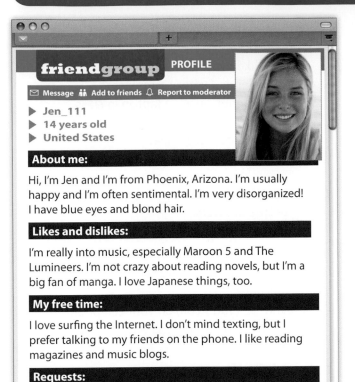

friendgroup PROFILE

✉ Message 👥 Add to friends 🔔 Report to moderator

▶ Jen_111
▶ 14 years old
▶ United States

About me:

Hi, I'm Jen and I'm from Phoenix, Arizona. I'm usually happy and I'm often sentimental. I'm very disorganized! I have blue eyes and blond hair.

Likes and dislikes:

I'm really into music, especially Maroon 5 and The Lumineers. I'm not crazy about reading novels, but I'm a big fan of manga. I love Japanese things, too.

My free time:

I love surfing the Internet. I don't mind texting, but I prefer talking to my friends on the phone. I like reading magazines and music blogs.

Requests:

I really want to meet sbdy 13–16 years old, but nbdy over 16, pls. I'm not too worried about your nationality, but I want sbdy who enjoys chatting on instant messenger.

○ Glossary

sbdy = somebody nbdy = nobody pls = please

1 Read the profile and answer the questions.

1 What adjectives describe Jen's character?
2 What does she like?
3 What does she read in her free time?
4 How does she want to communicate?

2 Study the profile and complete the key phrases. What follows these key phrases: a noun, verb + -ing, or both?

> **KEY PHRASES ○ Expressing likes and dislikes**
>
> I'm ¹___ into … .
> I'm ²___ crazy ___ … .
> I'm a ³___ ___ of … .
> I like / love / enjoy / prefer / hate … .
> I don't mind … .
> I'm not too ⁴___ ___ … .

3 Write six true sentences using the key phrases in exercise 2.

I love listening to hip-hop.

Language point: Capital letters and punctuation

4 Find capital letters, commas, and apostrophes in the text. Then complete the rules with the words in the box.

> contractions lists names

○ RULES

Capital letters: Use capital letters at the beginning of a sentence and for ¹___, nationalities, and countries: Simon, Austrian, Switzerland.

Commas: Use commas in ²___: I like hip-hop, rock, pop, and classical music.

Apostrophes: Use apostrophes for ³___: I'm (= I am), can't (= can not), don't (= do not).

5 Correct the sentences using capital letters, commas, periods, and apostrophes.

1 my names leo and i live in texas ✗
2 im really into german and spanish ✗
3 i love watching soccer tennis basketball and auto racing on tv ✗

6 **ACTIVATE** Follow the steps in the writing guide.

> **○ WRITING GUIDE**
>
> **A TASK**
>
> Write your Internet profile.
>
> **B THINK AND PLAN**
>
> 1 Think of two adjectives to describe you.
> 2 What do you look like?
> 3 What things do you like and dislike?
> 4 What do you do in your free time?
> 5 Who are you interested in meeting? What nationalities?
> 6 What languages or other things do you want to learn?
>
> **C WRITE**
>
> Copy the headings from Jen's profile. Then write your profile. Use the key phrases.
>
> **D CHECK**
>
> • capital letters   • commas in lists
> • apostrophes

Vocabulary

1 Match 1–5 with a–f. There is one word that you do not need.

1	bus	a	ring
2	ID	b	phone
3	MP3	c	pass
4	key	d	card
5	cell	e	watch
		f	player

2 Complete the sentences with the words in the box.

> group   Internet   magazines   music
> rules   shopping

1 Do you play in a ___?
2 I don't read ___.
3 It's against the ___ to take pictures.
4 He always surfs the ___.
5 I go ___ on the weekends.
6 When do you listen to ___?

Language focus

3 Complete the sentences using the simple present form of the verbs in brackets.

1 He ___ things. (collect)
2 I ___ swimming. (not go)
3 You ___ friends after school. (not meet)
4 She ___ the Internet in the evening. (not surf)
5 They ___ hip-hop. (listen to)
6 We ___ DVDs in English. (watch)

4 Write true simple present sentences using the adverbs of frequency in the box.

> never   hardly ever   sometimes   often
> usually   always

1 I / play soccer / on the weekends
2 I / walk / to school
3 I / meet friends / on Saturdays
4 I / go swimming / on Sundays
5 I / go to the movies / with my parents
6 I / listen to music / at school

5 Write simple present questions. Then write true short answers.

1 you / like / rock music
2 your friends / wear / sunglasses
3 your teacher / use / a laptop in class
4 you / live / in Europe
5 your friends / live / near you
6 you / carry / an ID card at school

6 Complete the simple present questions. Then write true answers.

1 What languages ___ (you / study)?
2 Where ___ (you / keep) your money?
3 When ___ (you / arrive) at school every morning?
4 Who ___ (you / call) on your cell phone?
5 When ___ (you / go) to bed?

Communication

7 Match 1–5 with a–f to make key phrases. There is one part that you do not need.

1	I'm really	a	fan of hip-hop.
2	I can't	b	about hip-hop.
3	I'm a big	c	into hip-hop.
4	I'm not crazy	d	stand hip-hop.
5	I love	e	listening to hip-hop.
		f	to hip-hop.

Listening

8 🔘 1.10 Listen to the dialogue and write *true* or *false*. Correct the false sentences.

1 Layla always loses things.
2 They're allowed to use cell phones at their school.
3 Layla doesn't use her cell phone in school.
4 Chris looks in Layla's bag.
5 Layla keeps a wallet in her bag.

1 Read the texts. Then match paragraphs 1–4 with photos A–D.

MY COLLECTION FOR 2100
BY JAMIE HILL

In here are objects and pictures which show my life today. It's a history lesson for you!
DON'T OPEN BEFORE 2100!

1 This is my cell phone. I always have it with me. It has all my pictures and music on it, and I use it to surf the Internet, too. I spend a lot of time talking with my friends on my phone. It's my favorite possession.

2 This is a Twilight DVD. There are four books, and there are movies, too. It's a story about vampires, and I think it's fantastic.

3 This is me on my skateboard. Skateboards are popular right now. People use them to travel or do tricks. There's a great skateboard park in town. Sometimes it's dangerous, but it's lots of fun.

4 These are my keys and my wallet. I have a student card, and a bus pass, so I can travel cheaply. The money is in dollars. People in the U.S. use dollars. I need these things every day, but I often lose them!

2 Make a poster of your *Collection for the future*. Follow the steps in the project checklist.

> ○ **PROJECT CHECKLIST**
>
> **1** Think of four things for your collection. Think of objects or people that are interesting and popular. Use your own ideas or choose ideas, such as: things that you use, activities that you do every day, a book that you like, a famous person that you like, a person in your family, your favorite possessions, or food or drink that you like.
>
> **2** Use your own pictures, or find a picture of each object or person on the Internet or in a magazine.
>
> **3** Write a short text for each picture. Explain what the picture is.
>
> **4** Stick your pictures and texts on some paper. Write a title and your name.

3 Exchange your *Collection for the future* with the rest of the class. Who has an interesting collection?

Home

Start thinking

1 What furniture is in your bedroom?
2 Are there famous houses in your country?
3 Do you help your parents at home?

Aims

Communication: I can ...

- describe the position of objects.
- understand advertisements and postcards.
- describe what is happening.
- talk about helping at home.
- contrast present actions with routines.
- make requests and compromises.
- describe my ideal home.

Vocabulary

- At home
- Housework

Language focus

- Present continuous: affirmative and negative
- Present continuous: questions
- Simple present and present continuous
- *and, but, because*

Reach Out Options

Extra listening and speaking

Finding things

⟹ Page 89

Curriculum extra

Language and literature: Poetry

⟹ Page 97

Culture

Homes in the U.S.

⟹ Page 105

Vocabulary puzzles

At home; Housework

⟹ Page 113

VOCABULARY ■ At home
I can describe the position of objects.

1 Which things in the box are **not** in the picture on page 19?

> table   chair   sofa   cupboard   lamp   picture   desk
> bookcase   mirror   bed   armchair   shower
> microwave   dresser   closet   washing machine   bath

2 Choose the odd word out for each room.

bedroom   bed   (sofa)   closet   dresser
1 **dining room**   table   chair   closet   picture
2 **living room**   microwave   lamp   armchair   picture
3 **kitchen**   cupboard   chair   bed   microwave
4 **bathroom**   mirror   lamp   bath   shower

(Pronunciation /ə/ ⟹ Workbook page 90)

3 🔘 1.16 Complete the sentences about the picture. Listen and check.

> ~~behind~~   between   in front of   near   next to
> on   under

There's a desk **behind** the bed.
1 There's an armchair ___ the TV and the table.
2 There are pictures ___ the bed.
3 There's a cupboard ___ the TV.
4 There are balls ___ the bed.
5 There's a small table ___ the TV.
6 There's a bed ___ the desk.

4 Look at the picture again and correct the sentences.

There's a truck **behind** the bicycles. ✗ near
1 There are pictures **in front of** the family. ✗
2 There are books **under** the dresser. ✗
3 There's a bed **on** the pictures and the desk. ✗
4 There's a table **between** the armchair. ✗
5 There's a TV **under** the armchair. ✗

5 **ACTIVATE** Look at the picture and match key phrases 1–4 with a–d. In pairs, play the *Memory game* on page 19.

> **KEY PHRASES ◯ Finding things**
>
> 1 Where's the table?   a They're behind the TV.
> 2 Where are the bicycles?   b No, there isn't.
> 3 Is there a mirror?   c Yes, there's one on the bed.
> 4 Is there a ball?   d It's in front of the TV.

(Is there an armchair?)   (Yes, there's one near the TV.)

> ◯ *Finished?*
> **Make anagrams of some of the words from exercise 1.**
> RESWHO = shower

Our home:
An American family and its possessions

Memory game

Look at the picture. Write five questions about where things are. Close your book. Then ask and answer your questions with a partner. What can you remember?

See celebrity homes ... in style

The *Classic Car Company* offers a three-hour tour of celebrities' homes for up to five people.

We don't use a bus! We give tours of Los Angeles in a classic Cadillac car. We visit about thirty different celebrities' homes in Los Angeles. Don't forget your camera!

We also:
- pick you up from your hotel,
- give you drinks in the car.

Price $395

☏ 800-789-9575

POSTCARD

Hi Ellie,

We're having a great time in the U.S. Right now, I'm sitting in a Cadillac convertible on Mulholland Drive in Hollywood! You can see everything in Los Angeles from here.

We're doing a tour of celebrity homes in a private car. It's my mom's birthday present from Dad. She loves movies.

Right now, we're outside Britney Spears's house. It's really big and it looks like a traditional Mediterranean villa. I think I can see her living room at the front of the house. There are lots of windows, so she has a great view of Los Angeles!

There's a big balcony, but Britney isn't sitting outside. She isn't living here right now. Our driver said Britney is in London. She's looking for a vacation home there!

Love,

Jen

1 Do you want to visit the home of a famous person? Which person's home and why?

2 Look at the advertisement. What does the *Classic Car Company* offer?

3 🔘 1.17 Read and listen to the advertisement and the postcard. Write *true* or *false*. Correct the false sentences.

1 Five people can go on the tour.
2 The tours start on Mulholland Drive.
3 You need to take something to drink.
4 Ellie is taking the tour right now.
5 Ellie's mom organized the tour.
6 Britney Spears isn't at home right now.

4 BUILD YOUR VOCABULARY Match words from the text 1–5 with their definitions a–e.

1	view	a	old style
2	traditional	b	a space on the outside of a house
3	windows	c	what you can see
4	balcony	d	you look through these
5	vacation home	e	an extra home

5 ABOUT YOU Ask and answer the questions.

1 Is your home modern or old?
2 Do you have a balcony or a garden?
3 Are there lots of windows in your home?
4 What is the view from your home?
5 Do some people have vacation homes in your country? Where?

I can describe what is happening.

1 Complete the sentences from the text on page 20 with the words in the box. Then choose the correct words in the rules.

> 're having   isn't living   'm sitting
> is looking

We **¹**___ a great time in the U.S.
I **²**___ in a Cadillac convertible.
She **³**___ here right now.
She **⁴**___ for a vacation home there!

○ **RULES**

1 We use the present continuous to talk about **habits / actions in progress**.
2 We make the present continuous with **verb / be** and the *-ing* form of the verb.

(More practice ⟹ Workbook page 17)

2 Find two more examples of the present continuous in the reading texts on page 20.

STUDY STRATEGY ○ **Finding spelling rules**

3 Write the *-ing* form of the verbs. Check your answers in the text on page 20. Then complete the spelling rules with words 1–5.

| 1 do | 3 live | 5 look |
| 2 sit | 4 have | |

○ **RULES**

1 **Most verbs:** add *-ing*: **doing**, ___
2 **Verbs that end in *-e*:** delete *-e* and add *-ing*: ___, ___
3 **Verbs that end in a short vowel and a consonant:** double the consonant and add *-ing*: **stopping**, ___

4 🔘 1.18 Listen to the sounds and complete the sentences using the present continuous form of the verbs in the box.

> call   cry   run   sleep   ~~wash~~   write

He**'s washing** his hands.
1 She ___.
2 He ___ an e-mail.
3 They ___.
4 The woman ___ her friend.
5 The baby ___.

5 Look at the picture and complete the sentences using the present continuous form of the verbs in the box.

> climb   describe   listen   ~~look~~   not look
> not rain   run   sleep   take

Two teenage girls **are looking** in a mirror.
1 A dog ___ near the house.
2 The driver ___ the house.
3 The tourists ___ to the driver.
4 The actor ___ into his house.
5 The teenage girls ___ at the house.
6 It ___.
7 Some tourists ___ pictures.
8 The boy ___ the wall.

6 **ACTIVATE** Write three true and three false sentences about the people in the picture. Then close your book. Listen to your partner's sentences and say if they are true or false.

(The dog is running.)

(False. The dog is sleeping.)

○ *Finished?*
Find five pictures in the book. Write a sentence about each picture using the present continuous.
page 14: *Shaun is showing Leah a basketball T-shirt.*

1 🔘 1.19 Check the meaning of the words in the box and complete the table. You can use some words more than once. Then listen and check.

> breakfast / lunch / dinner   out the trash
> the car   the dog for a walk   the floor
> the ironing   grocery shopping   ~~the table~~
> the vacuuming   the dishes   your bed
> your room

clear	make	do	go	clean	take	wash
the table						

2 Work in pairs. Do the questionnaire and compare your scores. Do you agree?

3 🔘 1.20 Listen to Jack and Megan. Choose the correct answer.

1 Jack and Megan are ...
   a brother and sister.   **b** friends.

4 🔘 1.20 Listen again and choose the correct answers.

1 Jack is reading a ___.
   a comic book   **b** magazine   **c** book
2 Megan ___ makes her bed.
   a always   **b** sometimes   **c** never
3 ___ always goes grocery shopping.
   a Megan   **b** Megan's mom
   c Megan's dad
4 ___ enjoys cooking.
   a Jack   **b** Megan   **c** Jack and Megan
5 Megan ___ doing the dishes.
   a hates   **b** doesn't mind   **c** loves
6 Megan's answers are mostly ___.
   a a   **b** b   **c** c

5 ACTIVATE Work in pairs. Take turns to mime housework activities in exercise 1. Guess what your partner is doing.

> You're making breakfast.

> Yes, I am.

Are you helpful around the house?

Do you help at home? Or do your parents do everything? Answer the questions.

1 How often do you make your bed?
   a I always make it in the morning.
   b I usually make it, but not always in the morning.
   c I never make my bed.
2 How often do you clean your room?
   a I always clean it on the weekend.
   b I don't often clean it.
   c I never clean it. Another person cleans it.
3 Who goes grocery shopping in your family?
   a I often go with my parents.
   b I occasionally go, but I don't enjoy it.
   c I never go grocery shopping. My parents do it.

4 Do you ever make lunch or dinner at home?
   a I often make lunch or dinner for my family.
   b I sometimes make lunch when I'm at home alone.
   c I never make lunch or dinner. I can't cook!
5 What do you do after dinner?
   a I always clear the table, do the dishes, and take out the trash.
   b I usually clear the table and I sometimes do the dishes.
   c I watch TV.
6 Do you help with the cleaning at home?
   a I often clean the floor and do the vacuuming.
   b I occasionally do the vacuuming, but I hardly ever clean the floor.
   c I never clean anything.

KEY

Mostly a – Your parents must be very happy because you're very helpful.
Mostly b – You sometimes help at home, but you don't really enjoy it. Try to help a little more.
Mostly c – You're not helpful at all. You think you live in a hotel!

Present continuous: questions

1 Match questions 1–3 with answers a–c. Then complete the rules.

1 Is Megan talking to Jack?
2 What are Jack and Megan doing?
3 Is Jack reading a comic book?

a No, he isn't.
b Yes, she is.
c They're doing a questionnaire.

> **○ RULES**
>
> 1 We ask about actions in progress using the question form of the ___.
> 2 We make short answers with a pronoun and the auxiliary verb ___.

(More practice ⇨ Workbook page 19)

2 Order the words to make questions.

where / sitting / is / best friend / your
Where is your best friend sitting?
1 in a chair / the teacher / sitting / is
2 learning / why / you / English / are
3 are / working / your parents
4 doing / your parents / are / what
5 this class / enjoying / are / you
6 talking / your teacher / to / who is

3 Work in pairs. Ask and answer the questions in exercise 2.

(Where is your best friend sitting?)

(She's sitting next to me.)

Simple present and present continuous

4 Study the examples. Then write *simple present* or *present continuous*. Complete the rules.

I walk to school every day. ¹___
He's reading a magazine now. ²___

> **○ RULES**
>
> 1 We use the ___ for actions in progress.
> 2 We use the ___ for routines or repeated actions.

(More practice ⇨ Workbook page 19)

5 Complete the telephone conversation with the simple present or present continuous form of the verbs in parentheses.

Elise	Hello.
Maria	Hi, Elise. It's Maria. What **are you doing** (do) right now?
Elise	I ¹___ (watch) *Celebrity Tours* on TV. It's about famous people's houses and possessions.
Maria	I ²___ (love) that program! I usually ³___ (watch) it every week.
Elise	The presenter ⁴___ (look) at Jay-Z and Beyoncé's cars right now. Beyoncé usually ⁵___ (drive) a 1959 Rolls-Royce. Take a look!
Maria	I can't. My parents ⁶___ (watch) something different.
Elise	Oh, no!

6 **ACTIVATE** Write simple present and present continuous questions using the words in the box and your own ideas. Then ask and answer the questions with a partner.

> are   does   what   dinner   your sister
> you   the dishes   why   talk to
> who   your parents   how often   go
> grocery shopping   when   make   where
> your brother   study

(How often does your sister make dinner?)

> **○ *Finished?***
> **Write a puzzle about some students in your class.**
> *She's wearing jeans and a blue T-shirt. She plays tennis and she gets good grades in English. Who is she?*

Mom	Leah, can you clean your room, please?
Leah	Yes, but later, OK? I'm busy right now.
Mom	Come on, Leah. What are you doing?
Leah	I'm watching something on TV. It's really good.
Mom	Leah! You need to clean your room now!
Leah	Please, Mom! Is it OK if I do it later?
Mom	You always say that, Leah. When?
Leah	I'll do it in ten minutes. I promise.
Mom	I suppose so, but please don't forget to do it!
Leah	OK! OK!

1 Look at the picture. What is Leah's mom saying?

2 ▶ 1.21 Listen to the dialogue. What does Leah's mom want Leah to do?

3 Find the key phrases in the dialogue. Who says them?

> **KEY PHRASES ○ Making requests and compromises**
>
> 1 Can you (**clean** your **room**), please?
> 2 **Yes**, but **later**, OK?
> 3 I'm **busy** right now.
> 4 I'll **do** it in (**ten minutes**).
> 5 I **suppose** so … .

4 ▶ 1.22 Listen and repeat the key phrases. Stress the words in bold. Why do we stress words?

5 ▶ 1.23 Listen to the sentences. What are the stressed words?

1 This article is really interesting. (2 words)
2 Sorry, I don't have time now. (2 words)
3 I'm helping Dad in the kitchen. (2 words)
4 Can you do your homework? (1 word)
5 I'm watching something on TV. (2 words)

6 Work in pairs. Practice the dialogue. Pay attention to the stressed words.

7 Work in pairs. Practice mini-dialogues using the key phrases.

do your homework / play a computer game

> Can you do your homework, please?

> I'm playing a computer game right now.

1 get dressed / chat on the Internet
2 make your bed / listen to my MP3 player
3 help Dad with the grocery shopping / talk on my cell phone
4 go to bed / write an e-mail

8 **ACTIVATE** Study the dialogue. Change the words in blue and practice your new dialogue with your partner. Use the ideas in exercise 7 or your own ideas.

WRITING ● A perfect place to live
I can describe my ideal home.

2

MY IDEAL HOME

A Here we are in my ideal home. It's a modern apartment near downtown. It's quite small, but it has everything. It has a kitchen and a living room. It also has three large bedrooms, each with bathrooms. The living room has a nice balcony and you can see the cathedral from it.

B Today, we're all at home. My mom and dad are sitting outside on the balcony. They're reading. My sister is in the kitchen. She's making lunch. I'm in my bedroom. I have a new laptop and I'm buying some cool games on the Internet.

C My favorite room is the living room. It has a big sofa and a really modern TV. There's a DVD player next to the TV. I like being in this room because it's relaxing.

1 Read the model text and match topics 1–3 with paragraphs A–C.

1 Adrian's favorite room
2 Description of Adrian's ideal home
3 What's happening now

2 Read the model text again and complete the key phrases with one or two words.

> **KEY PHRASES ○ Describing a place**
>
> 1 ___ a modern apartment, ___ downtown.
> 2 ___ three large bedrooms ... .
> 3 You ___ the cathedral from it.
> 4 ___ a DVD player next to the TV.
> 5 My ___ is the living room.
> 6 I ___ in this room because ... .

Language point: *and, but, because*

3 Study the words in blue in the text. Then complete the rules with *and, but,* or *because.*

> **○ RULES**
>
> 1 We use ___ to contrast two ideas.
> 2 We use ___ to give additional information.
> 3 We use ___ to give a reason.

4 Complete the sentences with *and, but,* or *because.*

1 There's a table, ___ there isn't a chair.
2 There are two pictures ___ a mirror.
3 My bedroom is my favorite room ___ it has all my things in it.

5 **ACTIVATE** Follow the steps in the writing guide.

> **○ WRITING GUIDE**
>
> **A TASK**
>
> Write about your ideal home.
>
> **B THINK AND PLAN**
>
> 1 What sort of house is it?
> 2 Where is it?
> 3 What rooms does it have?
> 4 Does it have a balcony or a yard?
> 5 Can you see anything special from the house, like a cathedral or the ocean?
> 6 Where is everyone right now? What are they doing?
> 7 What's your favorite room? What furniture does it have? Why do you like it?
>
> **C WRITE**
>
> Use *and, but,* and *because* and the key phrases.
> **Paragraph 1: Description**
> **Paragraph 2: What's happening now**
> **Paragraph 3: Favorite room**
>
> **D CHECK**
>
> • spelling and punctuation
> • present continuous verbs
> • use of *and, but,* and *because.*

Vocabulary

1 Choose the odd word out in each group.

1 kitchen   bedroom   shower   bathroom
2 view   desk   lamp   chair
3 window   table   bookcase   cupboard
4 armchair   chair   sofa   mirror
5 bath   mirror   shower   microwave
6 closet   bed   lamp   washing machine

2 Choose the correct verbs.

1 **do / make / clear** your bed
2 **clear / do / take** the table
3 **take / clean / make** your room
4 **clear / wash / make** the car
5 **take / go / make** grocery shopping
6 **take / clean / do** out the trash

Language focus

3 Look at the picture. Complete the sentences with the present continuous form of the verbs in the box.

clean   make   not do   not stand   take

1 Mom ___ dinner.
2 The boy ___ the ironing.
3 The cats ___ on the chair.
4 The girl ___ the floor.
5 Dad ___ the dog for a walk.

4 Write questions using the present continuous. Then look at the picture in exercise 3 and write short answers.

1 Mom / wear / a dress
2 the cats / sleep
3 the boy / watch / TV
4 the children / listen to / music
5 the girl / work

5 Complete the sentences. Use the simple present or present continuous form of the verbs.

1 Carl always ___ (make) his bed in the morning, but he ___ (not clean) his room!
2 ___ you ___ (watch) this movie? I ___ (not enjoy) it.
3 I ___ (help) at home every day. Right now I ___ (make) dinner for my family.
4 Right now, my Canadian cousins ___ (stay) at our house. They always ___ (visit) us in New York in the summer.

Communication

6 Complete the mini-dialogues with the words in the box.

it's   is there   there is   where

Tom   ¹___ an e-mail for me?
Sophie   Yes, ²___.
Tom   ³___ 's the laptop?
Sophie   ⁴___ on my bed.

I'm   I suppose   is it   can you

Dad   ⁵___ do the dishes, please?
Josh   ⁶___ busy right now. ⁷___ OK if I do them later?
Dad   ⁸___ so, but don't forget to do them!

Listening

7 🔘 1.24 Listen to Ellen and Daisy and look at the sentences. Write *true* or *false*. Correct the false sentences.

1 Ellen is speaking on her cell phone.
2 Ellen's brother is talking to his cousin.
3 Daisy doesn't like Steve Dunton.
4 Ellen's brother is in the living room.
5 Ellen's dad is doing the vacuuming.
6 Steve and Ellen's brother are talking about a girl called Stacy.

Listening

1 Look at the pictures and answer the questions.

1 Where do you think Alan is on vacation?
2 Where do you think Bess is?
3 Do you think Alan is having a good time?

2 🔘 1.25 Listen to Alan and Bess talking about Alan's vacation. Which is Alan's hotel room?

3 🔘 1.25 Listen again and complete the sentences with one, two, or three words.

1 Bess doesn't really like museums, but she does like ___.
2 Alan's hotel is in the center of ___.
3 The view from Alan's room is of a ___.
4 Alan's parents go to bed at ___.
5 Bess is ___ her room right now.
6 Lily is coming on ___.
7 Lily, Bess, and Alan usually go to the ___ on Friday nights.
8 Bess wants Alan to send her some ___.

Speaking

4 Work in pairs. Prepare a conversation. Imagine that person A is on vacation in another country.

1 Where is A?
2 Is A enjoying his / her vacation?
3 What is A doing?
4 Where is A staying?
5 What does A do in the evenings?
6 What is B doing now?

5 Have a conversation. Use your ideas in exercise 4 and the chart below to help you. One of you is A and one of you is B. When you finish, change roles.

A *Hi!*

B Reply and ask about the vacation.

A Reply.

B Ask about the hotel.

A Describe the hotel.

B *What do you do in the evenings?*

A Reply and ask what B is doing.

B Reply.

A Ask about another friend.

B Reply.

Writing

6 Write an e-mail to a friend. Tell your friend about your vacation. Begin like this:

Hi, ...,
We're in ... and I think it's really nice.

3

Looking back

Start thinking

1 Do you have a good memory?
2 What can you do if you have a photographic memory?
3 What did you do last weekend?

Aims

Communication: I can ...

- describe feelings and events.
- understand a text about people with good memories.
- talk about past events in my life.
- talk about important life events.
- talk about past events.
- talk about experiences in the past.
- describe an event in the past.

Vocabulary

- Adjectives: feelings and events
- Milestones

Language focus

- *was, were*
- Simple past
- Time expressions and *ago*
- *there was*, *there were*

Reach Out Options

Extra listening and speaking

An event in the past

⇨ Page 90

Curriculum extra

Language and literature: Folk stories

⇨ Page 98

Culture

Teenage years

⇨ Page 106

Vocabulary puzzles

Adjectives: feelings and events; Milestones

⇨ Page 114

VOCABULARY ■ Adjectives: feelings and events

I can describe feelings and events.

1 Think about your first memory and answer the questions.

1 How old were you?
2 Were you happy?
3 Where were you?
4 Who was with you?

2 🔘 1.31 Match pictures 1–7 with the phrases in the box. Then listen and check.

> a nervous teenager   a lonely dog   a lucky girl
> a naughty child   a scary movie   an upset baby
> a cute baby

3 Choose the correct words.

1 On my first day of school I was very **nervous / lucky**.
2 I was in a car accident when I was a baby. But I was OK. I was very **lucky / lonely**.
3 I remember a trip to the circus. I didn't like it. The clowns were really **scary / cute**!
4 I remember my baby brother on the day he was born. He was very **cute / lonely**.
5 I was six. My mom was **upset / lucky** because I was very **scary / naughty**.
6 I was at a party, but I didn't know anyone. I was **naughty / lonely**.

4 Do the *How good is your memory?* quiz with a partner. Then look at the key. Do you agree?

5 **ACTIVATE** Write true sentences. Compare your answers with your partner.

I'm sometimes upset when *I argue with my best friend.*
1 My ___ is cute.
2 I think ___ are scary.
3 When I'm naughty, my parents ___.
4 I'm usually nervous when ___.
5 When I'm feeling lonely, I ___.

> ⭕ *Finished?*
> **Choose a picture in exercise 2 and write about it.**
> *The teenager is nervous. She doesn't like tests. She doesn't understand ...*

How good is your MEMORY?

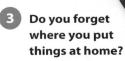

1 **Look at the pictures for ten seconds. Then cover the pictures and repeat the words. How many can you remember?**
a All or most of them.
b About half of them.
c Not many.

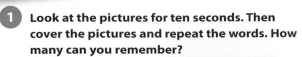

2 **Can you remember any jokes?**
a Yes! I know lots of jokes.
b I know a few.
c No. I always forget them.

3 **Do you forget where you put things at home?**
a I never lose anything.
b Sometimes. But I usually find them again.
c Yes, I do. I get really upset sometimes.

4 **Is it easy for you to remember facts for tests?**
a I'm lucky. I remember everything I read.
b It's hard. I forget some things.
c I always forget everything I read.

5 **Were you naughty as a young child?**
a Yes, I remember my teachers and parents were often angry with me.
b I don't think so. I'm not sure.
c I've no idea! I can't remember anything.

6 **Do you remember your first day of school?**
a Yes, I do. I was really nervous.
b I think so. It was a long time ago. I was about five.
c I can't remember last week, so I really can't remember when I was young.

7 **Do you remember the first birthday party you went to?**
a Yes, I remember it well. It was a very happy day.
b I remember a party, but I don't know if it was the first one.
c I can't remember any parties.

8 **When you wake up, do you remember your dreams?**
a I usually remember them. I love dreams.
b I only remember some dreams, like scary ones.
c I wake up and forget them immediately.

9 **Don't look back! How many things in question 1 can you remember?**
a 7–8 things.
b 4–6 things.
c 1–3 things.

KEY
Mostly a = You have an excellent memory! You can remember things now and in the past. This is a useful skill for learning languages! You're very lucky.
Mostly b = Your memory is good, but not great. With practice, it can be better.
Mostly c = Your memory isn't great. Our advice: start writing a diary! Don't forget!

Meet the MEMORY MASTERS

Some people call Stephen Wiltshire "the human camera." Stephen was in a helicopter for twenty minutes, above London, and then he drew pictures of the city from memory. Stephen wasn't born in London and he doesn't know the city, but in twenty minutes, he memorized hundreds of buildings. His pictures weren't perfect, but they were very detailed.

Most people don't have a photographic memory like Stephen. In fact, the maximum number of things people can usually remember from a list is about six or seven. But it is possible to train your brain.

For example, Mahavir Jain, from India, memorized 18,000 words and definitions from an English dictionary. His English tests were easy after that, and now he owns three English schools.

People also try to memorize pi. For most people at school, 3.142 is enough, but Akira Haraguchi, from Japan, once recited 100,000 digits of pi in sixteen hours. He started at 9:30 a.m. on a Tuesday and finished at 1:28 a.m. the next day. It was a record.

There are also memory superstars. Dominic O'Brien was first interested in memory after he left school and he started to train his memory. In 1991, he won the World Memory Championships. He was World Memory Champion seven more times between 1992 and 2001. In 2002, Dominic memorized the order of cards in fifty-four packs of playing cards. That's 2,808 cards! The world record was 2,704 cards. When he repeated the cards, Dominic was wrong only eight times!

1 Study the numbers for fifteen seconds. Then close your book. How many can you remember?

> 12   65   8   31   18   74   55   4   90   57

2 ● 1.32 Read and listen to the text. Which four people does the text mention? How are they similar?

3 Read the text again. Write *true* or *false*. Correct the false sentences.

1 Stephen Wiltshire lives in London.
2 Stephen drew a helicopter.
3 Mahavir Jain learned 18,000 words and their meanings.
4 Akira Haraguchi learned 100,000 digits of pi in 16 hours.
5 Dominic O'Brien was World Memory Champion seven times.

4 **BUILD YOUR VOCABULARY** Complete the sentences with the words or phrases in blue in the text.

1 Can you ___ what the homework is tonight?
2 I ___ ten English irregular verbs every night.
3 The girl said the poem ___.
4 My mom almost has a ___. She sees something and remembers it.
5 I have a terrible ___. I forget everything.
6 My friend once ___ the alphabet from Z to A.

5 **ABOUT YOU** Ask and answer the questions.

1 Do you have a good memory? Give an example.
2 How do you remember English vocabulary?
3 What things do you often forget?
4 What things do you memorize?
5 How often do you recite something? What is it?
6 Is it good to have a photographic memory? Why / Why not?

LANGUAGE FOCUS ■ *was, were*
I can talk about past events in my life.

1 Look at the text on page 30 and complete the sentences with the words in the box. Then complete the rules using the correct form of *was* and *were*.

> ~~was~~   was   wasn't   was   were

Dominic O'Brien **was** the champion in 2001.

1 Stephen's pictures of London weren't perfect, but they ___ very detailed.
2 Stephen Wiltshire ___ born in London.
3 "___ the world record 2,704 cards?" "Yes, it was."
4 "How many times ___ Dominic wrong?" "He was wrong only eight times."

◯ RULES

1 In affirmative sentences, we use *was* or ___.
2 In negative sentences, we use ___ or *weren't*.
3 In *yes / no* questions, we use ___ / *were* + pronoun + the verb in the base form.
4 In short answers, we use *yes, / no,* + pronoun + ___ / *wasn't* or *were / weren't*.

> More practice ⇨ Workbook page 25

2 🔘 1.33 Complete the sentences using the correct form of *was* and *were*. Then listen and check.

Barack Obama **was** President of the U.S. in 2009.

1 The World Cup champion in 2010 ___ Spain.
2 Michael Jackson ___ an American singer.
3 DVDs ___ popular in 1980.
4 Robert Pattinson and Kristen Stewart ___ in the *Twilight* movies.
5 I ___ at school in 2001.

3 Work in pairs. Ask and answer questions about the sentences in exercise 2 using *was* and *were*.

> Was Barack Obama President of the U.S. in 2009?

> Yes, he was.

4 Complete the questions with the words in the box. Then ask and answer the questions with your partner.

> What was   What were   When was
> Were you   ~~Was the~~   Where were

Was the weather good last Thursday?

1 ___ the last birthday in your family?
2 ___ in a school play when you were young?
3 ___ the names of your first school friends?
4 ___ your favorite toy when you were young?
5 ___ you yesterday morning?

> Was the weather good last Thursday?

> Yes, it was!

5 ACTIVATE Work in pairs. Talk about past events using *was* and *were* and the words in the boxes.

> When   What   Who   Where

> your last meal?
> you on the weekend?
> your homework?
> you at seven o'clock in the morning?
> your first teachers?
> your last tests?
> the weather like yesterday?
> your first school?
> your last visit to the dentist?

> When was your last meal?

> It was at half past seven.

◯ *Finished?*
Write five quiz questions about famous people.
Was William Shakespeare an English writer?

1 ● 1.34 Choose the correct verbs. Then listen and check.

1 have / do / **become** a professional
2 **have** / go / start a child
3 be / do / **have** born
4 graduate / win / **get** a job
5 **leave** / go / do to school
6 move / get / **learn** to drive
7 go / **leave** / do school
8 **take** / win / go a test
9 **buy** / do / go a house
10 **graduate** / go / leave from college
11 **win** / get / graduate a competition
12 **leave** / do / have home
13 **move** / start / have to another country
14 **start** / go / do a company
15 **get** / do / go married
16 **become** / go / have rich

2 ● 1.35 Work in pairs. Match the names to the pictures. Then listen and check.

> Angelina Jolie   Beyoncé   Bill Gates
> Brad Pitt   Kate Moss   Tom Cruise
> Keira Knightley   Serena Williams

> I think picture F is Angelina Jolie.

3 ● 1.36 Listen and complete the sentences with one or two words.

1 Kate Moss ___ model when she was fifteen.
2 Brad Pitt went to college to ___ a journalist.
3 Angelina Jolie bought ___ in New Orleans in 2007.
4 Bill Gates didn't ___ from college, but he became very rich.
5 Keira Knightley got ___ on television at the age of nine.
6 Tom Cruise learned to ___ before he was twenty.
7 Beyoncé got ___ to rapper Jay-Z.
8 Serena Williams ___ to school.

4 ACTIVATE Work in pairs. Ask and answer questions about life events.

What age do people usually ...
1 ... first go to school?
2 ... leave school?
3 ... graduate from college?
4 ... leave home?
5 ... get married?
6 ... learn to drive?

> What age do people usually go to school?

> Children first go to school at the age of 5.

WHO'S WHO?

A

B

C

D

E

F

G

H

1 Look at the verbs in the box and find the past forms in exercise 3 on page 32. Then complete the table.

> become buy get go ~~graduate~~
> learn ~~leave~~

Past forms	
Regular (add -d or -ed)	**Irregular**
graduate – graduated	leave – left

Pronunciation: Past tense -ed endings ⇨ Workbook page 90

2 Complete the sentences with the words in the box. Then answer questions a–c.

> didn't go   played   taught

1 Serena first ___ tennis at the age of four.
2 She ___ to school.
3 Serena's father ___ her at home.

a Which sentence has a simple past form of a regular verb?
b Which sentence has a simple past form of an irregular verb?
c Which sentence is in the simple past negative?

3 Match questions 1–3 with answers a–c.

1 When did Bill Gates start a company?
2 Where did Angelina and Brad buy a house?
3 Did Brad Pitt go to college?

a In New Orleans.
b Yes, he did.
c In 1975.

4 Study the examples in exercises 2 and 3. Then choose the correct words in the rules.

> ⬤ **RULES**
>
> 1 The simple past form of a verb is the **same / different** for all persons.
> 2 In negative sentences, we use *didn't* + the verb in the **base form / simple past**.
> 3 In questions, we use (question word) *did* + noun or pronoun + the verb in the **base form / simple past**.

More practice ⇨ Workbook page 27

STUDY STRATEGY ⬤ **Learning irregular verbs**

5 Follow instructions 1–3.

1 Find past tense verbs in the text on page 30. Add them to the table in exercise 1.
2 When you find a new verb, check the irregular verbs list in your Workbook. Then add the verb to the table.
3 Memorize five irregular verbs every week.

6 Complete the text using the simple past form of the verbs in parentheses.

A MEMORABLE LIFE

Elizabeth Blackwell was born in 1821 in Britain. At the age of 11, her family [1]___ (move) to New York.

In those days, women [2]___ (not work) and they [3]___ (not go) to college, but Elizabeth [4]___ (want) to become a doctor. The medical schools [5]___ (not want) a woman student, but Elizabeth [6]___ (graduate) with the highest grade in her class and she [7]___ (become) the first woman doctor in the U.S.

7 **ACTIVATE** Complete the questions using the verbs in the box. Then ask and answer with a partner.

> buy   get   graduate   have   leave

1 When ___ your dad ___ school?
2 When ___ your parents ___ married?
3 When ___ your parents ___ their first child?
4 When ___ your parents ___ their first car?
5 ___ your parents ___ from college?

> When did your dad leave school?

> He left school in 1981.

> ⬤ *Finished?*
> **Find the simple past forms of the verbs in exercise 1 on page 32. Add them to your table in exercise 1 on this page.**

SPEAKING ● Your weekend
I can talk about experiences in the past.

Shaun	Hey, Maya. How was your weekend?
Maya	Not bad, thanks.
Shaun	What did you do?
Maya	I went shopping on Saturday and bought a DVD. What about you?
Shaun	I watched a soccer game.
Maya	Cool. I love soccer.
Shaun	Really? When did you last go to a soccer game?
Maya	Three weeks ago.
Shaun	What did you see?
Maya	I saw the U.S. national team against Mexico.
Shaun	Wow! Was it good?
Maya	Yes, it was really exciting. The U.S. won 2–1.

1 (●) 1.37 Listen and read the dialogue. What soccer game did Maya see?

2 Match key phrases 1–4 with answers a–d. Then practice the dialogue with a partner.

> **KEY PHRASES ○ Talking about an experience**
>
> 1 How was your weekend?
> 2 What about you?
> 3 When did you last go to the movies?
> 4 Was it good?
>
> a A month ago.
> b Yes, it was.
> c It was great.
> d I went to the movies.

Language point: Time expressions and *ago*

3 Complete the time expressions using *ago*. Where do we put *ago* in time expressions?

last year = **a** year **ago**
1 7:30 a.m. = ___ hours ___
2 last Tuesday = ___ days ___
3 yesterday = 24 ___ ___
4 on Saturday = ___ days ___
5 last week = a week ___

4 Imagine that today is Monday. Order the time expressions. Start with the most recent.

> a year ago   ~~an hour ago~~   last Monday
> on Saturday   yesterday morning

1 an hour ago

(More practice ⇨ Workbook page 27)

5 Work in pairs. When did you last do these activities? Invent mini-dialogues. Use time expressions and *ago*.

> go to the movies   watch a DVD
> celebrate a friend's birthday
> watch a soccer game   have a party

(When did you last go to the movies?)

(I went to the movies two days ago.)

(Was the movie good?) (Yes, it was very funny!)

6 **ACTIVATE** Look again at the dialogue in exercise 1. Change the words in blue and practice your new dialogue with a partner. Use the ideas in exercise 5 and your own ideas.

WRITING ● A past event
I can describe an event in the past.

3

A day to remember

I remember my cousin's wedding six months ago. It was Saturday and there wasn't a cloud in the sky. It was a very memorable day.

First, a lot of people came to our house. At twelve o'clock, we went to the church for the ceremony, and after that, we went to a hotel. We had lunch there, and then the party started at about six o'clock. There was an amazing band and everybody danced. There weren't any problems. Finally, at about midnight, we went home.

There were about a hundred people at the wedding. I remember my grandmother clearly because she had a really strange hat! It was a really great day and I felt very happy.

1 Read the model text about a memorable day. Then order the key phrases.

KEY PHRASES ○ Linking events

a After that, everybody went to a hotel.
b Finally, everyone went home.
c First, a lot of people went to Kate's house.
d At twelve o'clock, we went to the church.
e Then the party started.

1 c 2 … 3 …

Language point: *there was, there were*

2 Match 1–4 with a–d. Then translate the sentences.

1 There was   a a cloud in the sky.
2 There wasn't   b an amazing band.
3 There were   c any problems.
4 There weren't   d about a hundred people.

3 Complete the sentences with the affirmative or negative of *there was*, or *there were*.

There was a cute boy at the party. His name was Tom.

1 ___ a big chocolate cake at Jen's birthday. It was delicious!
2 We had fruit and ice cream at Charlie's birthday because ___ a cake.
3 ___ fireworks on New Year's Eve. I loved them.
4 ___ any interesting people at the party. I went home early.

4 **ACTIVATE** Follow the steps in the writing guide.

○ WRITING GUIDE

A TASK

Write three paragraphs about one of these events:
• Your first day at school
• A birthday
• A party

B THINK AND PLAN

1 What and where was the event?
2 What happened first?
3 What happened after that?
4 Who do you remember clearly?
5 How did you feel that day?

C WRITE

Paragraph 1: Introduction: *I remember …*
Paragraph 2: Event: *First, …*
Paragraph 3: Conclusion: *There were … people …*

D CHECK

• simple past forms
• linking words
• *ago*

Vocabulary

1 Choose the correct words.

1 I was a **cute / lucky / nervous** child. I didn't want to talk to other children.
2 We saw a very **upset / cute / scary** movie yesterday.
3 My **scary / lonely / lucky** number is four.
4 My younger brother is very **lonely / naughty / cute**. He never listens to Mom.
5 He was **nervous / upset / lucky** because he didn't pass his test.
6 Her cat is very small and beautiful. It's **nervous / cute / lonely**!

2 Complete the phrases with the verbs in the box. There is one verb you do not need.

> become buy go graduate have move take

1 ___ rich
2 ___ to school
3 ___ a child
4 ___ a house
5 ___ a test
6 ___ from college

Language focus

3 Complete the dialogue using the affirmative or negative forms of *was* and *were*.

Rob What is your first memory, Sally?
Sally I ¹___ in our kitchen at home and I ²___ really upset.
Rob Why?
Sally I wanted some ice cream, but there ³___ any.
Rob How old ⁴___ you?
Sally I ⁵___ very old – maybe four or five.
Rob ⁶___ your parents there?
Sally No, they ⁷___. My sister ⁸___ with me.

4 Complete the sentences using the simple past form of the verbs in the box.

> pass graduate not like not learn live meet

1 My grandmother ___ to drive when she was young. She ___ her driving test last year!
2 My dad ___ my mom in college. They ___ from college in 1988.
3 Our English teacher ___ in California for three years, but he ___ Los Angeles.

5 Write questions for the answers using the simple past.

1 "When ___ to Spain?"
"He moved to Spain two years ago."
2 "___ to the movies last week?"
"Yes, I did. I went to the movies last Friday."
3 "Who ___ at the party?"
"I met Thomas's brother. He's cute."
4 "What ___ ?"
"She said there isn't any homework tonight!"
5 "___ the party?"
"They left the party because they were tired."

Communication

6 Complete the dialogue with the words in the box.

> a year ago How was I played It was
> it was Was it What about When did

Sam ¹___ your weekend?
Ruby ²___ great.
Sam What did you do?
Ruby I stayed at home and watched TV! ³___ you?
Sam ⁴___ tennis with my brother.
Ruby ⁵___ good?
Sam Yes, ⁶___. I won!
Ruby Cool. I like tennis.
Sam Really? ⁷___ you last play tennis?
Ruby About ⁸___. I like *watching* tennis. I don't like *playing* tennis!

Listening

7 🔊 1.38 Listen to James and his dad talking about James's grandfather. Then complete the text.

James's ¹___ didn't go to college. He left ²___ at sixteen and his first job was in a ³___. He started his own ⁴___ after James's ⁵___ Sally was born. A year later, James's grandfather bought his first ⁶___ and his first car. James's ⁷___ was a nervous driver. James thinks his ⁸___ is also a nervous driver.

1 Read Katrina's paragraphs. Then match them with headings a–d.

   a Their lives together   **c** My grandparents
   b Our family now   **d** The 1950s

My family history poster

by Katrina Hill

1 _____

My mother's parents, Alice and Joe, are both from Texas, but they live in Florida now. Joe was born in Houston in 1937, then his family moved to Dallas, and Alice was born in 1940 in Dallas. Alice and Joe went to the same school, but they didn't meet.

2 _____

Life was hard in the 1940s, when Joe and Alice were children, but things changed in the 1950s. "Rock and roll" music started, and TV became very popular. Alice remembers her teenage years as a wonderful time.

3 _____

Joe left school in 1951, and got a job as a construction worker. Alice became a nurse. They met at Doctors Hospital, after Joe had an accident at work. They went out together for three years and then they got married in 1961.

4 _____

Alice and Joe had five children, and now, they have nineteen grandchildren. When we have big family parties, there are over thirty people! I love my big family. I always have friends to talk to.

2 Make a family history poster. Follow the steps in the project checklist.

> ### ◯ PROJECT CHECKLIST
>
> **1** Decide who in your family you want to write about (uncles / aunts, grandparents, great-grandparents).
>
> **2** Find out more about their lives. Ask other people in your family about them, or ask them if they are still alive.
>
> **3** Collect family pictures, or use the Internet to find pictures of times which were important in the lives of the people you are writing about.
>
> **4** Organize your ideas:
> - early life
> - the time he / she / they lived in
> - main life events
> - their connection to your family life now
>
> **5** Make a poster of your family history. Stick the pictures next to your writing and give each paragraph a heading.

3 Exchange your family history poster with your classmates. What did they write about?

4

Dare!

Start thinking

1 What is a daredevil?
2 Why is Niagara Falls famous?
3 Do you want to explore the world? What do you want to see?

Aims

Communication: I can ...

- make and respond to suggestions.
- read about the history of a famous place.
- describe what was happening at a past event.
- talk about places in the world.
- invent a story about a world trip.
- talk about amazing experiences.
- write about a rescue.

Vocabulary

- Prepositions: movement
- Geographical features

Language focus

- Past continuous: affirmative and negative
- Past continuous: questions
- Simple past and past continuous
- *when*, *while*, *as soon as*

Reach Out Options

Extra listening and speaking

Directions

⇨ Page 91

Curriculum extra

Natural science: Geological formations

⇨ Page 99

Culture

Adventure sports in New Zealand

⇨ Page 107

Vocabulary puzzles

Prepositions: movement; Geographical features

⇨ Page 115

VOCABULARY ■ Prepositions: movement

I can make and respond to suggestions.

1 Match pictures 1–9 with the prepositions in the box.

> across   around   down   into   off   over   through   under   up

2 Read the *Daredevils quiz* and choose the correct prepositions.

3 🔘 2.02 Do the quiz. Then listen and check your answers.

4 Work in pairs. Describe the pictures in exercise 1 using the verbs in the box and a preposition.

> climb   ride   fall   jump   run   swim   walk

1   *climb up*

5 Complete the sentences with the prepositions in exercise 1.

Did he sail **across** the Atlantic Ocean?
1 He fell ___ the bridge, but he was OK. He was lucky.
2 I like skiing ___ big mountains!
3 Can you climb ___ a fifty-meter high tree?
4 Kate is crazy. She ran ___ the freezing ocean in December!
5 They're sailing ___ the Greek islands.
6 We rode our bikes ___ the forest. There were trees all around us.

6 Study the key phrases. Then complete them with *Yes* or *No*.

> **KEY PHRASES ◯ Making and responding to suggestions**
>
> Why don't we (jump into the river)?
> 1 ___, it looks (exciting).
> 2 ___, it's too (scary).
>
> Let's (ride our bikes across Arizona over our vacation).
> 3 ___, that sounds (boring).
> 4 ___, that's a (good) idea!

7 **ACTIVATE** Work in pairs. Make suggestions. Use the key phrases and the verbs and prepositions in exercises 1 and 4.

> Shall we climb over that wall?

> Yes, it looks easy.

> ◯ *Finished?*
> **Choose five places and invent adventures there.**
> Climb up a mountain in the Alps and ski down it ...

DAREDEVILS QUIZ

A

B

C

1 Some people like jumping **off** / **around** / **up** buildings, bridges, and monuments (photo A). This activity is called …
- **a** base jumping.
- **b** crazy jumping.
- **c** basic flying.

2 Dave Kunst walked **into** / **around** / **down** the world. He walked …
- **a** 1,100 kilometers.
- **b** 2,200 kilometers.
- **c** 23,200 kilometers.

3 Drivers in the Paris–Dakar rally drive **down** / **across** / **under** the Sahara Desert. The Sahara is in …
- **a** Asia.   **b** Africa.   **c** Australia.

4 Downhill mountain bikers ride **under** / **down** / **into** huge mountains (photo B). They use …
- **a** mountain bikes.
- **b** hill bikes.
- **c** BMX bikes.

5 Martin Strel, from Slovenia, swam **through** / **off** / **along** the entire length of the Amazon River in 66 days. He swam …
- **a** 526 kilometers.
- **b** 15,260 kilometers.
- **c** 5,265 kilometers.

6 Firewalkers walk **around** / **across** / **into** hot coals (photo C). The coals are …
- **a** 50°C.   **b** 500°C.   **c** 5,000°C.

7 Stunt motorcyclists can jump **into** / **through** / **over** fifty or more cars. The record distance for a motorcycle jump is …
- **a** 18 meters.
- **b** 58 meters.
- **c** 98 meters.

1 Read the text. Which daredevils does it mention?

2 🔘 2.03 Match headings 1–4 with paragraphs A–E. Then listen and check.

A new tightrope champion   C

1 A lady at the falls
2 Tightrope hero
3 The end of stunts at Niagara
4 Facts about Niagara Falls

3 Read the text again. Write *true* or *false*. Correct the false sentences.

1 Tourists go to Niagara Falls now.
2 Blondin watched and copied Farini.
3 Farini became popular with his new stunts.
4 It wasn't a surprise for the crowd when Annie Taylor survived.
5 Only one or two people do stunts at Niagara now.

4 BUILD YOUR VOCABULARY Complete the sentences with the words in blue in the text.

1 My __ and __ are all athletes. I admire them.
2 He's very __ and brave. He doesn't think anything is scary.
3 I saw some __ on TV. They were sailing around the world.
4 He can do some new __ on his bike.
5 This place is fantastic. The mountains are __.

5 ABOUT YOU Ask and answer the questions.

1 What do you think of the daredevils in the text?
2 Which movies that you've seen have stunts? Describe them.
3 What places in your country are spectacular?
4 Who are your heroes and heroines? Why?
5 Do you know anyone who's daring? In what way?

NIAGARA FALLS – DON'T LOOK DOWN!

A At Niagara Falls, on the border between the U.S. and Canada, the Niagara River suddenly falls more than fifty meters. Every hour, 2.5 million liters go over the waterfalls. Niagara Falls is popular with tourists and, in the past, it was also popular with daredevils. Three of the most famous were The Great Blondin, Signor Farini, and Annie Taylor.

B In 1859, Blondin walked across Niagara Falls eight times. Once, he cooked eggs while he was standing on the tightrope. Another time, he nearly fell into the river while he was carrying a man on his back. That day, a man named William Hunt was at Niagara with his girlfriend. As they were watching Blondin, Hunt decided to invent stunts which were more spectacular and daring than Blondin's. He changed his name to Signor Farini and began to practice.

C In 1860, a crowd went to see Farini at Niagara. He was walking along his tightrope when he stopped and climbed down a thirty-meter rope to a boat. He had a drink, then climbed up the rope again and continued walking. He was the new king of the falls.

D There were many heroes of Niagara, and also some heroines. In 1901, Annie Taylor became the first woman to go over the falls in a barrel. People were waiting for forty minutes before Annie's helpers opened the barrel. People weren't expecting to see Annie alive, but in fact she survived.

E Many others survived stunts at the falls in barrels, balls, or simply a bathing suit, but a lot of people also died. These days, daredevil acts are prohibited there and there is a maximum fine of $10,000.

LANGUAGE FOCUS ■ **Past continuous: affirmative and negative**
I can describe what was happening at a past event.

1 Complete the sentences with the words in the box. Check your answers in the text on page 40. Then choose the correct words in the rule.

> was carrying   was standing
> were watching   weren't expecting

1 He ___ on the tightrope.
2 He ___ a man on his back.
3 They ___ Blondin.
4 People ___ to see Annie alive.

> **○ RULE**
>
> The past continuous describes **a finished action / an action in progress** in the past.

(More practice ⇨ Workbook page 33)

> **STUDY STRATEGY ○ Using the rules boxes**

2 Study the spelling rules for *-ing* forms on page 21. Then write the *-ing* form of the verbs.

1 drive   3 jump   5 ride
2 run   4 fly   6 swim

3 Complete the text using the past continuous form of the verbs in parentheses.

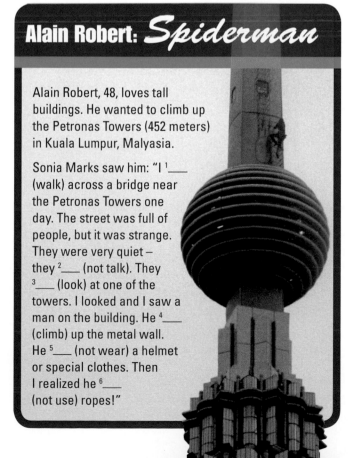

Alain Robert: *Spiderman*

Alain Robert, 48, loves tall buildings. He wanted to climb up the Petronas Towers (452 meters) in Kuala Lumpur, Malyasia.

Sonia Marks saw him: "I ¹___ (walk) across a bridge near the Petronas Towers one day. The street was full of people, but it was strange. They were very quiet – they ²___ (not talk). They ³___ (look) at one of the towers. I looked and I saw a man on the building. He ⁴___ (climb) up the metal wall. He ⁵___ (not wear) a helmet or special clothes. Then I realized he ⁶___ (not use) ropes!"

4 Write true sentences about today. Use the affirmative or negative form of the past continuous.

I / sleep / at 9 a.m.
I wasn't sleeping at 9 a.m.

1 my friends / play / soccer at 6 a.m.
2 I / sit / in a car at 8:15 a.m.
3 we / listen / to the teacher five minutes ago
4 my friends and I / talk / at 8:45 a.m.
5 I / sleep / at 5 a.m.
6 it / rain / before school

5 **ACTIVATE** Work in pairs. Look at the pictures and imagine you saw the event. Describe what was happening. Use the questions to help you.

1 What were you doing when you saw this?
2 What was the stunt person doing?
3 Who was watching?
4 What was the crowd doing?

(Pronunciation: Weak forms ⇨ Workbook page 91)

> **○ Finished?**
> **Imagine that you are one of the daredevils in this unit. Write the story of one of your stunts.**
> I was at Niagara Falls. I was walking across the falls on a tightrope …

1 Death Valley

2 ___ Erie

3 the South ___

4 the Rocky ___

5 the Black ___

6 the Amazon ___

7 the Sahara ___

8 Niagara ___

9 the Dead ___

10 the Pacific ___

1 🔊 2.04 **Complete the names of places 1–10 with the words in the box. Then listen and check.**

> Desert Falls Forest Lake Mountains
> Ocean Pole River Sea ~~Valley~~

2 **Work in pairs. Complete the sentences with the words in exercise 1.**

1 The Andes are ___.
2 It never rains in the Atacama ___.
3 There isn't any land at the North ___.
4 The Atlantic ___ is between the U.S. and Europe.
5 There's a Red ___, a Black ___, and a Yellow ___.
6 The Amazon is a ___ and a ___.

3 🔊 2.05 **Listen to Layla and Emily's story. Which trip did they make?**

a From the North Pole to the United States.
b From Greenland to the North Pole.
c From the North Pole to the Equator.

4 🔊 2.05 **Choose the correct answers. Listen again and check.**

1 How long was Layla and Emily's trip?
  a 700 kilometers   b 1,700 kilometers
  c 17,000 kilometers
2 Where were they skiing when Layla fell through the ice?
  a the United States   b Greenland
  c Panama
3 How far did they sail to North America?
  a 400 kilometers   b 4,000 kilometers
  c 14,000 kilometers
4 What was the problem while they were riding their bikes?
  a There were storms.   b It was too cold.
  c It was too hot.
5 How did they get to Quito?
  a They walked and climbed.
  b They rode their bikes.   c They sailed.

5 **ACTIVATE Work in pairs. Write clues about a geographical feature which you know in your country, or other countries. Then test your partner.**

> This is a famous desert in Asia.

> Is it the Gobi Desert?

> Yes, it is!

Past continuous: questions

1 Match questions 1–6 with answers a–f. Then complete the rule.

1 Were you skiing?
2 Was she riding a bike?
3 Were they sailing?
4 What were they doing?
5 Who was waiting?
6 Where were you waiting?

a In Quito.
b They were traveling.
c No, they weren't.
d My dad.
e Yes, I was.
f No, she wasn't.

◯ RULE

We form past continuous questions with (question word) + ___ + subject + *-ing*.

> More practice ⇨ Workbook page 35

2 Write questions and answers about Emily and Layla's trip using the past continuous.

Was Emily **traveling** with her parents? (travel) **No, she wasn't.**

1 ___ Emily and Layla ___ in Greenland? (ski)
2 ___ Layla ___ in the Atlantic Ocean? (swim)
3 Where ___ they ___ ? (ride their bikes)
4 Where ___ they ___ to? (sail)
5 Who ___ ___ for them in Quito? (wait)

3 Write questions using the past continuous. Then ask and answer the questions with a partner.

1 what / you / do / at 6:30 last night
2 you and your family / have / breakfast at 7:30 a.m.
3 what / your parents / do / at 8:30 a.m. yesterday
4 you / walk / to school at 8 o'clock
5 where / you / sit / at 9:30 yesterday morning
6 who / sit / next to you / in your English class / last week

Simple past and past continuous

4 Study the examples. Then complete the rules with *simple past* and *past continuous*.

While they were skiing across Greenland, Layla fell through the ice.

They were skiing across Greenland when Layla fell through the ice.

◯ RULES

1 We use the ___ to describe past actions that were in progress.
2 We use the ___ to interrupt the action that was in progress.
3 We often use *when* before the ___ and *while* before the ___.

> More practice ⇨ Workbook page 35

5 Complete the sentences. Use the simple past and the past continuous in each sentence.

He **wasn't looking** (not look) when he **fell** (fall) through the ice.

1 He ___ (swim) when he ___ (see) the shark.
2 They ___ (meet) while they ___ (walk) near the river.
3 Peter ___ (have) an accident while he ___ (ski).
4 I ___ (not wear) a bicycle helmet when I ___ (fall off) my bike.
5 They ___ (not sleep) when we ___ (call) them.

6 **ACTIVATE** Work in pairs. Imagine you went on a world trip. Talk about what you did using the simple past and past continuous. Use the verbs in the box and your own ideas.

> climb   ride (a bike)   meet   see   speak
> stay   swim   travel   visit   walk
> sail   buy

> I saw the pyramids while I was traveling along the Nile River.

◯ *Finished?*

Imagine you are interviewing an explorer about an adventure. Write six interview questions. Use the simple past and past continuous. Then write the explorer's answers.

How did you feel while you were sailing across the Atlantic?

SPEAKING ● Expressing interest
I can talk about amazing experiences.

Leah Did you take this picture, Shaun?
Shaun Yes, do you like it?
Leah Yeah. But what was happening?
Shaun ¹ This skateboarder was jumping over a table.
Leah Oh! That's amazing! ² Where were you when you saw that?
Shaun I was ³ on vacation in Madrid. These kids were doing tricks on their skateboards.
Leah Really? ⁴ Why were they doing that?
Shaun ⁵ It was a show.
Leah Did you try it?
Shaun You're kidding! ⁶ I can't skateboard.
Leah Well, it's a great picture. Well done!
Shaun That's very kind of you.

1 What are Shaun and Leah looking at? What do you think they are saying?

2 🔊 2.06 Cover the dialogue and listen. Did Shaun try skateboarding?

3 🔊 2.07 Cover the dialogue and complete the key phrases. Listen, read, and check. Practice the intonation of the key phrases. How do we use intonation to show surprise?

> **KEY PHRASES ○ Expressing interest**
>
> Oh! That's ¹___!   ³___ done!
> Really?   That's ⁴___ ___ of you.
> You're ²___!

4 Invent five amazing experiences. Use the ideas in the box and your own ideas. Compare your ideas with a partner. Remember to use intonation to show surprise.

> climb up Everest   dive with sharks
> fly a helicopter   meet Lionel Messi
> see Alicia Keys
> skateboard down some stairs
> swim across the English Channel
> visit Hollywood and Las Vegas

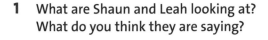

I jumped off a bridge last year.

Really? That's amazing!

5 Look at the photo of the diver. Replace the numbered phrases in blue in the dialogue with phrases a–f. Practice a dialogue about the diver with your partner.

a This diver was diving from a ten-meter board.
b I don't like the water.
c in Barcelona with my dad. We were visiting sites from the 1992 Olympics.
d There was an international diving competition.
e What were they doing at that pool?
f Where did you take it?

6 **ACTIVATE** Look again at the dialogue in exercise 2. Change the words in blue and practice your new dialogue with a partner. Use the ideas in exercise 4.

A Brave Rescue

[1]The rescue happened while we were on vacation in Australia last year. It was really amazing and [2]I was lucky to get a picture of it.

I was walking along the beach with my family. There were a lot of big waves, and it was raining and windy. There was a man with a dog. He was walking on some rocks. [3]Suddenly, a huge wave crashed into them. The man was OK, but I couldn't see his dog. After a few minutes, we saw the dog again. It was swimming, but it went under the water a few times. Two surfers on the beach were watching as well. [4]As soon as they saw the dog, they swam towards it on their surfboards.

[5]When they reached the dog, they put it onto a surfboard. Then they swam back to the beach. [6]They were very brave because the ocean was dangerous.

1 Read the model text. Match information 1–6 with summaries a–f.

  a how the rescue ended
  b what the writer thought about the rescuers
  c how the rescue started
  d where the rescue happened
  e how the writer felt about his / her picture
  f how the accident happened

2 Complete the key phrases with the words in the box.

> after   as soon as   suddenly   when
> while

KEY PHRASES ◯ Linking events

1 The rescue happened ____ we were on vacation.
2 ____ they reached the dog, they put it onto a surfboard.
3 ____ a few minutes, we saw the dog again.
4 ____ they saw the dog, they swam out to it.
5 ____, a huge wave crashed into them.

Language point: *when, while, as soon as*

3 Choose the correct words.

1 I saw the shark **while** / **as soon as** I was swimming.
2 **As soon as** / **While** I saw it, I swam away.
3 **When** / **While** he saw the accident, he went to help.

4 **ACTIVATE** Look at the photo of the helicopter rescue in the writing guide below. Then follow the steps in the writing guide.

◯ WRITING GUIDE

A TASK

Imagine that you took the picture of the helicopter rescue. Write a story with the title *A Brave Rescue*.

B THINK AND PLAN

1 When and where did the rescue happen?
2 What happened to the person on the stretcher?
3 How did the rescuers know about the accident?
4 Why was the rescue dangerous?
5 How did the rescue end?

C WRITE

Paragraph 1: Introduction
The rescue happened ...
Paragraph 2: The people and the rescue
There was ... / There were ...
Paragraph 3: The end and your opinion
The rescuers ...

D CHECK

• *when, while, as soon as*
• *there was, there were*
• simple past and past continuous verbs
• linking words

Vocabulary

1 Choose the correct words.

1 I was swimming **down** / **across** / **up** a lake.
2 Don't fall **through** / **up** / **off** the bridge!
3 Walk **over** / **across** / **through** the door.
4 I'm climbing **up** / **under** / **into** a mountain.
5 The cat jumped **over** / **through** / **in** the chair!
6 We ran **down** / **off** / **into** the mountain.

2 Match descriptions 1–6 with the words in the box.

> desert   valley   forest   lake   ocean   pole

1 The point at the north or south of the world.
2 An area of water with land all around.
3 A place with lots of trees.
4 A low area of land between mountains.
5 A place where it hardly ever rains.
6 A very big area of water where ships sail.

Language focus

3 Write an affirmative and a negative sentence for each picture using the past continuous form of the verbs.

1 ride his bike / run

2 read a magazine / listen to music

3 clean the floor / clear the table

4 swim / climb

5 make his bed / do his homework

6 watch a DVD / play in a group

4 Look at the pictures in exercise 3. Write questions and short answers using the past continuous.

1 he / wear / a helmet
2 she / read / a book
3 they / help / at home
4 the cat / jump / over a tree
5 he / listen / to music
6 they / sing / in a group

5 Complete the sentences. Use the simple past and the past continuous in each sentence.

1 She ___ (fall) off her bike while she was ___ (ride) down the mountain.
2 We ___ (take) a test when the fire ___ (start).
3 I ___ (see) Katy while I ___ (sit) on the bus.
4 You ___ (not listen) when the teacher ___ (call) your name.

Communication

6 Complete the mini-dialogues.

1 "You did a great trick on your skateboard."
"Really? That's very k_ _d of you."
2 "Why d_ _'t we visit Niagara Falls?"
"Yes, it l_ _ _s amazing."
3 "I visited Death Valley last year."
"You're k_ _ _ _ _g ! That's a_ _ _ _ _g !"
4 "L_ _'s watch *Avatar*." "No, it s_ _ _ _s boring."

Listening

7 ● 2.08 Listen to Lucy and Clare. Complete the sentences with one, two, or three words.

1 Lucy wants to go on vacation before ___.
2 Lucy went to Argentina ___ with her parents.
3 In the Andes Mountains, you can climb, swim, or go kayaking across ___.
4 Clare isn't a ___. She doesn't like dangerous sports.
5 Clare doesn't want to ___ across Chile because there are ___.
6 Clare likes reading books, ___, beaches, and sunny afternoons.

Listening

1 Look at the pictures and answer the questions.

  1 Where did Alan and Lily go last weekend?

  2 What do you think happened?

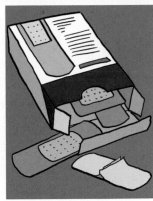

2 2.09 Listen to Alan, Bess, and Lily talking about last weekend. Which is the correct picture?

3 2.09 Listen again. Write *true* or *false*. Correct the false sentences.

  1 Bess's grandparents moved recently.

  2 Lily and Alan went walking around the lake.

  3 Lily hurt her leg on Sunday.

  4 The weather was good at the lake.

  5 Lily fell off her bike when she hit a dog.

  6 Alan rode into Lily's bike.

  7 Lily fell into the lake.

  8 The dog was jumping on Alan.

Speaking

4 Work in pairs. Prepare a conversation about last weekend. Imagine that person A had an accident.

  1 Where was A when he / she had the accident?

  2 What was he / she doing?

  3 What happened after the accident?

  4 How does he / she feel now?

5 Have a conversation. Use your ideas in exercise 4 and the chart below to help you. One of you is A and one of you is B. When you finish, change roles.

A Ask about B's weekend.

B Tell A about your weekend.

A Reply and say you had an accident.

B Ask about A's accident.

A Tell the story of your accident.

B Express interest.

A Say how you are feeling now.

B Suggest an activity for next weekend.

A Reply.

Writing

6 Write a postcard to a friend. Imagine you had an accident over the weekend. Explain how it happened. Begin like this:

Hi …,

How are you? Last weekend, I …

Unfortunately, I had an accident and …

5 Smart

Start thinking

1 Which composers, painters, and writers do you like?
2 What are you good at?
3 Which animals are intelligent?

Aims

Communication: I can ...

- say how much I know about a person.
- understand a text about child prodigies.
- talk about past and present abilities.
- describe the qualities of things.
- use comparative and superlative adjectives.
- compare ideas for a present.
- write a biography of a person.

Vocabulary

- Skills and people
- Adjectives: qualities

Language focus

- Ability: *can* and *could*
- Questions with *How...?*
- Comparative and superlative adjectives
- *should* and *must*

Reach Out Options

Extra listening and speaking
Buying tickets
⟹ Page 92

Curriculum extra
Natural science: Adapting to the environment
⟹ Page 100

Culture
National festivals
⟹ Page 108

Vocabulary puzzles
Skills and people; Adjectives: qualities
⟹ Page 116

VOCABULARY ■ Skills and people
I can say how much I know about a person.

1 Work in pairs. Do the *Smart kids quiz*.

2 ● 2.15 Complete the table with verbs and nouns from the *Smart kids quiz*. Then listen and check.

Skill (verb)	Person (noun)	Skill (verb)	Person (noun)
paint	painter	write	4 ___
compose	1 ___	win	5 ___
swim	2 ___	6 ___	programmer
3 ___	player	sing	7 ___

STUDY STRATEGY ○ Learning words in groups

3 ● 2.16 Writing groups of related words is a useful way of expanding your vocabulary. Complete the table with related words. Then listen and check.

Verb	Person	Noun
invent	inventor	invention
act	1 ___	2 ___
3 ___	4 ___	dancing
5 ___	cook	6 ___

⟮ Pronunciation: Word stress ⟹ Workbook page 91 ⟯

4 Which words in the box can be used in key phrase 1 and which can be used in phrase 2?

⟮ a little   a lot   anything   much ⟯

KEY PHRASES ○ Expressing knowledge

1 I know ___ about ... .   2 I don't know ___ about ... .

5 **ACTIVATE** Work in pairs. Talk about the people in the box using the key phrases in exercise 4.

⟮ Mark Twain   Ludwig van Beethoven   Cristiano Ronaldo
John Lennon   J.K. Rowling   William Shakespeare
Vincent van Gogh   Leonardo DiCaprio   Emma Watson ⟯

⟮ I don't know much about Mark Twain. ⟯

⟮ I think he was an American writer. ⟯

○ *Finished?*
Use a dictionary. Find five more words you can add to the *Verb* list in exercise 3. Then complete the *Person* and the *Noun* lists.

SMART KIDS QUIZ

Pablo Picasso was Spanish. He painted this when he was nine years old. Which of these painters was Spanish?

a Salvador Dalí
b Leonardo da Vinci
c Vincent van Gogh

The Brontë sisters were writers. They wrote stories and poems for each other when they were children. Which is not a Brontë novel?

a Jane Eyre
b Wuthering Heights
c Oliver Twist

Mozart started to compose music when he was five. Which of these people wasn't a composer?

a Ludwig van Beethoven
b Henry Ford
c Richard Wagner

Will Jenkins was the winner of a photography competition when he was eight. Which of these is a part of a camera?

a lens
b mouse
c printer

The swimmer Michael Phelps was fifteen when he competed in the Olympics in Sydney. Five months later, he broke the world record for 200 m butterfly. Which of these is not an Olympic sport?

a table tennis
b karate
c basketball

S. Chandra Sekhar started to program computers when he was seven years old. Which of these is not a computer language?

a Java
b C++
c Chinese

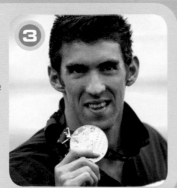

Judit Polgár played in international chess competitions when she was eight. Which of these is not a chess piece?

a prince
b king
c queen

Now a famous singer, Leona Lewis wrote her first song when she was twelve. In which TV competition did Leona sing?

a Big Brother
b The X Factor
c Survivor

1 What does *prodigy* mean? Do you know the names of any prodigies?

2 🔊 2.17 Read and listen to the text. Then choose the correct summary.

The author of the text describes:
a how different the life of a prodigy is.
b how prodigies study in college.
c how to become a prodigy.

3 Read the text again and complete the sentences with one, two, or three words.

Wendy Vo was very good at **languages**.
1 S. Chandra Sekhar went to college at the age ___.
2 Some parents like the same things as their ___.
3 Ainan Cawley's parents wanted him to start ___.
4 Parents can help child prodigies if ___ their children, but not push them too hard.
5 Albert Einstein had an IQ of ___.

4 BUILD YOUR VOCABULARY Study the text. Find and complete the phrases with the verbs in the box. You need to use some verbs more than once.

> break   start   make   take

1 ___ a record   4 ___ a decision
2 ___ a test   5 ___ friends
3 ___ a break   6 ___ college

5 ABOUT YOU Ask and answer the questions.

1 How often do you take English tests?
2 How often do you take a break when you study for tests?
3 Would you like to start college at your age? Why? Why not?
4 Did you make friends quickly in this class?
5 Do you want to break a record? What is it?
6 Which decisions are difficult for you to make?

PRODIGY!

Could you speak another language at the age of eight? At this age, Wendy Vo could speak eleven languages fluently. She couldn't brush her teeth by herself, though! Another child genius, S. Chandra Sekhar, could program a computer at seven. At ten, he took tests at the company Microsoft and two years later, he went to college.

Prodigies are children with incredible talents. They can do things that many adults can't do. Some scientists think prodigies are born with their talents. However, their parents usually help them. Sometimes children and parents have the same interests. For example, Mozart's father was a composer and Picasso's father was a painter.

Some parents of prodigies are very ambitious or strict. Ainan Cawley is a chemistry prodigy. At seven, his parents wanted him to start college! When János Starker, a famous cello player, was young, his mother taught their parrot to say, "Practice, János, practice!"

Clearly, life is sometimes difficult for prodigies. How do you make friends at college when you're twelve? And it's difficult to take a break when a parrot is shouting at you!

Psychologists believe that parents of prodigies need to help their children but not push them too hard. Two-year-old Elise Tan-Roberts' mom is a good example. Elise broke a record when she scored 156 on an IQ test. Albert Einstein's score was only 160! Elise's mother made an important decision about her daughter. She said, "Her IQ is really high, but if it goes down, we won't be upset."

LANGUAGE FOCUS ◼ Ability: *can* and *could* • Questions with *How ...?*
I can talk about past and present abilities.

Ability: *can* and *could*

1 Complete the sentences. Use the text on page 50 to help you.

They **can** do things that many adults ¹___.
Wendy Vo ²___ speak eleven languages.
She ³___ brush her teeth by herself.

(More practice ⇨ Workbook page 41)

2 Choose the correct words.

> ○ **RULES**
>
> 1 We use an infinitive **with** / **without** *to* after *can* and *could*.
> 2 The *he* / *she* / *it* form of *can* is **can** / **cans**.
> 3 The negative of *can* is **don't can** / **can't**.
> 4 We use *can* to talk about the **present** / **past**.
> 5 We use *could* to talk about the **present** / **past**.

3 Complete the sentences with the words in the box.

(can   can't   could   couldn't   couldn't)

1 Beethoven couldn't hear when he composed his 9th symphony, but he ___ imagine the music.
2 Agatha Christie ___ spell very well, but she wrote eighty detective books.
3 The actor Ben Affleck lived in Mexico when he was a teenager. Now he ___ speak English and Spanish.
4 Franklin D. Roosevelt had polio and ___ walk, but he became President of the U.S.
5 Beyoncé sings some of her songs in Spanish, but she ___ speak the language.

Questions with *How ...?*

4 Match 1–7 with a–g to make questions. Then ask and answer the questions with a partner.

1 How far can ...   a are in your class?
2 How strict is ...   b go to the movies?
3 How often do you ...   c do you drink?
4 How intelligent are ... d are you?
5 How many people ...   e you swim?
6 How much water ...   f your teacher?
7 How tall ...   g your friends?

5 Write questions for the sentences using *How ... ?* and the words in the box.

(far   fast   ~~high~~   long   long   many times)

Danny Way jumped seven meters high on a skateboard.
How high did Danny Way jump?
1 Samantha Druce, 12, swam 33.8 kilometers across the English Channel.
2 Jef Sarver played a guitar for forty-eight hours.
3 Yam Bhandari's hair is 2.9 meters long.
4 Chris Carr traveled at more than 600 kilometers per hour on a special motorcycle.
5 Ang Rita Sherpa climbed Mount Everest five times between 1983 and 1996.

(More practice ⇨ Workbook page 41)

6 **ACTIVATE** Work in pairs. Ask and answer questions about abilities. Use the ideas in the box and your own ideas.

How	far	can could	you	jump	? when you were ...?
	much			run	
	high			remember	
	many English words			swim	
	fast			speak	

(How far can you swim?)

(I can swim about two kilometers.)

> ○ *Finished?*
> **Write sentences about what you couldn't do in the past, but that you can do now.**
> When I was one I couldn't talk, but now I can speak two languages.

1 ● 2.18 Find pairs of opposite adjectives. Then listen and check.

> ~~artistic~~ aggressive common
> domesticated fast heavy intelligent

> light peaceful ~~practical~~ rare slow
> stupid wild

artistic – practical

2 Work in pairs. Write sentences about each animal using three adjectives from exercise 1. Use *not very*, *pretty*, *very*, and *really*.

Cat Cats are domesticated, pretty fast, and very common.

1 elephant   4 whale
2 dog   5 monkey
3 octopus

3 ● 2.19 Listen to Sophie and Joe talking about animals. Which animal that they talk about is **not** in the photos?

4 ● 2.19 Choose the correct words. Then listen again and check your answers.

1 Octopuses can remember people's **names** / **faces**.
2 Octopuses **can** / **can't** change color.
3 Elephants **can** / **can't** understand human language.
4 Dogs can understand a lot of **vocabulary** / **grammar**.

5 ● 2.19 Listen again and complete the sentences with one or two words.

1 The elephant is more ___ Joe.
2 Elephants are the most ___ animal.
3 ___ faster learners than elephants.
4 An elephant's brain is bigger than a ___ brain.
5 Sophie thinks her dog is the ___ on the planet.

6 ACTIVATE Work in pairs. Think of an animal. Then describe it using the adjectives in the box and in exercise 1. Can your partner guess your animal?

> horrible small boring interesting
> big nice beautiful

It's big, it's wild, and it's aggressive. It lives in forests.

Is it a bear?

1 Complete the table with comparative and superlative adjectives.

	Adjective	Comparative	Superlative
Short adjectives	fast	¹___	the fastest
	big	²___	the biggest
	rare	rarer	the rarest
	noisy	noisier	the ³___
Long adjectives	artistic	⁴___	the most artistic
	intelligent	more intelligent	⁵___
Irregular adjectives	good	better	the best
	bad	worse	the worst

2 Study the example sentences and the table in exercise 1. Then complete the rules with *the* and *than*.

The elephant is more artistic than I am.

An elephant's brain is bigger than a whale's brain.

Elephants are the most intelligent animal.

> **○ RULES**
>
> 1 We often use ___ after comparative adjectives.
> 2 We often use ___ before superlative adjectives.

3 Study the table in exercise 1 again. Complete the spelling rules and add examples.

Spelling rules		
Type of adjective	**Rule**	**Examples**
Most short adjectives	Add -er / -est	faster / ¹___
Short adjectives that end in -e	Add -r / -st	²___ / rarest
Short adjectives that end in -y	-y → -i + -er / -est	heavier / heaviest
Short adjectives that end in a short vowel and a consonant	Double the consonant and add -er / -est	³___ / biggest

More practice ⇨ Workbook page 43

4 Study the information. Then make sentences using comparative and superlative forms.

	Atlantic marlin	Common dolphin	Blue whale
Population	400,000	2–3 million	11,000
Length	4 meters	2.3 meters	25 meters
Speed	80 km/h	50 km/h	48 km/h
Weight	450 kg	100 kg	150,000 kg
Aggressive	!!!!	!!	!
Intelligent	★★	★★★★	★★★

Atlantic marlin (fast)
The Atlantic marlin is the fastest.
1 Atlantic marlin / blue whale (aggressive)
2 common dolphin (short)
3 Atlantic marlin / common dolphin (heavy)
4 blue whale / Atlantic marlin (rare)
5 blue whale (slow)
6 blue whale / Atlantic marlin (intelligent)

5 ACTIVATE Ask and answer questions about the animals in exercise 4 using comparative and superlative forms of the adjectives.

> long   fast   heavy   aggressive   slow
> intelligent   rare   short   common

Which animal is the rarest?

The blue whale is the rarest.

Which animal is longer than the Atlantic marlin?

The blue whale is longer than the Atlantic marlin.

> **○ *Finished?***
> **Write six quiz questions with comparative and superlative adjectives.**
> *Are humans more intelligent than rats?*

SPEAKING ○ Choosing a present

I can compare ideas for a present.

Shaun	I must be home at five o'clock, Maya. How long will you be?
Maya	Just a few minutes. I'm looking for a poster for my dad's birthday. He's into art.
Shaun	Can I see?
Maya	Yes. What do you think of this? It's by Picasso.
Shaun	It's OK. What about this one?
Maya	Who's it by?
Shaun	It's by van Gogh. It's called *Starry Night*.
Maya	This one's better. I like it.
Shaun	Me too. You should get him this one.
Maya	Do you think so?
Shaun	Yes, it's more interesting. The other one's sort of boring.
Maya	Yes, I think you're right. Thanks, Shaun.

1 Who are the most famous artists from your country? Do you have any posters of their work?

2 ● 2.20 Listen to the dialogue. Does Maya agree with Shaun about the posters?

3 ● 2.21 Listen to the key phrases. Then answer the questions.

> **KEY PHRASES ○ Choosing a present**
>
> 1 "He's into art."
> Who is "he"?
> 2 "Who's it by?"
> Who is the second painting by?
> 3 "This one's better. I like it."
> Which is "this one"?
> 4 "The other one's sort of boring."
> Which is "the other one"?

4 Work in pairs. Practice the dialogue.

Language point: *should* and *must*

5 Study the examples and complete the rules with *should*, *shouldn't*, *must*, and *may not*.

I must be at home at five o'clock.

You should get him this one.

We may not use our phones at school. It's against the rules.

You shouldn't buy that shirt. It's horrible!

> **○ RULES**
>
> We use ¹___ / ___ to talk about obligation and we use ²___ / ___ to give advice.

6 Complete the sentences with *should* or *must*.

1 Tom loves jazz. We ___ buy him this CD.
2 We ___ leave our MP3 players in our bags in tests.
3 In some countries you ___ carry your ID card all the time.
4 You're good at singing. You ___ join a band.

7 **ACTIVATE** Look again at the dialogue in exercise 2. Imagine that you're buying a present for a friend. Change the words in blue and practice your new dialogue with a partner. Use the ideas in the box and your own ideas.

> book   CD   clothes   jewelry
> bag   computer game   DVD

WRITING ● Biographies
I can write a biography of a person.

Mark Twain

A Mark Twain was an American writer. He was born in Missouri in 1835. He lived in the U.S. for his whole life. He died on April 21, 1910.

B By the age of sixteen, Mark Twain was writing articles for a small newspaper. He left Missouri two years later and traveled all over the U.S., from the east coast to the far west. He worked in many different jobs, but he became a journalist and writer in 1861.

C In total, he wrote thirteen novels and many short stories. He is most famous for the books *The Adventures of Tom Sawyer* and *Adventures of Huckleberry Finn*. His novels were funnier and more realistic than many other novels of the time.

D Now, students in high schools and colleges study his novels and there are many different movie and TV versions of his stories. There are also several Mark Twain museums in different parts of the U.S.

1 Read the model text. Then match headings 1–5 with paragraphs A–D. There is one heading that you do not need.

1 How Mark Twain started writing
2 Mark Twain's style of writing and his most famous books
3 Mark Twain's likes and dislikes
4 How Mark Twain is still famous today
5 A summary of Mark Twain's life

2 Study the model text and find the time expressions in blue. Then match 1–6 with a–f.

KEY PHRASES ○ Writing a biography

1	He was born in Missouri in …	a	April 21.
2	He lived in the U.S. for …	b	students study his novels.
3	By …	c	he left Missouri.
4	Two years later, …	d	his whole life.
5	He died on …	e	1835.
6	Now, …	f	the age of sixteen, he … .

3 **ACTIVATE** Follow the steps in the writing guide.

○ WRITING GUIDE

A TASK

Write a biography. Use the notes on Hergé or details about another writer you admire.

B THINK AND PLAN

1 Where and when was he born?
2 Where did he grow up?
3 When did he die?
4 Where did he study?
5 What did he do as a job?
6 What is his most famous character? How many books did he write?
7 Why were the books successful?
8 Is Tintin still famous? Why?

C WRITE

Paragraph 1: Summary of life
Hergé was born in …
Paragraph 2: Education and work
He studied at school in …
Paragraph 3: Most famous for …
His most famous cartoon character is …
Paragraph 4: How he is famous today
Today, the Tintin books …

D CHECK

• comparative and superlative forms
• time expressions

HERGÉ
writer and artist

BORN: Brussels, Belgium, 1907

REAL NAME: Georges Remi

LIVED: in Belgium, traveled all over the world

DIED: Brussels, Belgium, March 3, 1983

STUDIED: school in Brussels, good at all subjects except art

WORKED: 1927, as a cartoonist for a Belgian newspaper

MOST FAMOUS CHARACTER: Tintin (24 books) – about a young journalist and his dog, Snowy

QUALITIES OF HIS BOOKS: very detailed, exciting, funny characters

NOW: Tintin books are in 91 languages, Steven Spielberg is making movies of the books

Vocabulary

1 Complete the sentences with the correct form of the words in the box.

> compose   paint   dance   cook   write

1 J.K. Rowling became a ___ in 2003. In the next five years, she ___ five books.
2 Ludwig van Beethoven was a ___. He ___ some of the most famous classical music in the world.
3 My sister is a great ___. She can ___ flamenco, ballet, and salsa.
4 I'm a good ___. I often ___ dinner for my family.
5 Tom ___ pictures of animals. He's a great ___, and he wants to be an artist.

2 Complete the adjectives with *a, e, i, o,* and *u.* Then find pairs of opposites.

1 sl__w
2 d__m__st__c__t__d
3 st__p__d
4 l__ght
5 c__mm__n
6 __ggr__ss__v__

a p__ __c__f__l
b __nt__ll__g__nt
c w__ld
d r__r__
e h__ __vy
f f__st

Language focus

3 Complete the sentences with the words in the box.

> can   can't   could   couldn't
> how many   must   should

1 You ___ turn off cell phones during tests. It's one of the rules!
2 "___ you swim when you were four?"
"No, I ___. I learned when I was six."
3 "___ languages ___ your parents speak?"
"Only English. They ___ speak any other languages."
4 "Do you have any advice?"
"Yes, you ___ tell your teacher."

4 Write comparative and superlative sentences about the dogs.

	Whippet	Ridgeback	Saint Bernard
Weight	★★★	★★★★	★★★★★
Top speed	★★★★★	★★★	★★
Rare	★	★★★★★	★★
Aggressive	★	★★★★	★★

1 The Saint Bernard / rare / the Whippet
2 The Whippet / fast
3 The Saint Bernard / common / the Ridgeback
4 The Ridgeback / aggressive
5 The Ridgeback / rare
6 The Ridgeback / slow / the Whippet

Communication

5 Complete the dialogue with the words in the box.

> should   she's into   about this
> do you think   who's it   this one's

Rachel You know a little about classical music, Sue. What ¹___ of this CD?
Sue Beethoven's 1st Symphony? Yes, it's very good. Why are you asking?
Rachel I'm looking for a present for my mom's birthday. ²___ classical music.
Sue OK. ³___ better, I think.
Rachel ⁴___ by?
Sue Beethoven again. It's his 5th Symphony.
Rachel What ⁵___ one? His 9th symphony.
Sue No, you ⁶___ get her the 5th symphony.

Listening

6 2.22 Listen to the conversation and look at the sentences. Write *true* or *false.* Correct the false sentences.

1 Tom's parents think their house is too small.
2 Tom had a cat.
3 Tom likes taking dogs for a walk.
4 Martha thinks Tom should get a dog.
5 Tom is moving closer to school.
6 Tom is moving onto Martha's street.

1 Read Emily's *Celebrity quiz* and try to answer the questions.
Then match the quiz questions with the answers.

Lady Gaga

A celebrity quiz by Emily Roberts

HER LIFE

1 What is Lady Gaga's real name?
2 Is she the oldest child in her family?
3 How tall is Lady Gaga?

HER MUSICAL CAREER

4 Could she play the piano when she was five years old?
5 How old was she when she was composing her first songs?
6 What was her first big hit?

HER IDEAS

7 Where does her celebrity name come from?
8 Who are her heroes?
9 What is unusual about her?

ANSWERS

a She loves David Bowie and Freddie Mercury. "Glam Rock" music starts of the 1970s. She's also into the clothes designer Donatella Versace.
b Yes, she could. She learned to play when she was just four.
c She wears very unusual clothes and makeup.
d Just Dance from her 2008 album *The Fame*.
e A 1980s song by the band Queen, *Radio Ga Ga*.
f Stefani Joanne Angelina Germanotta.
g Only about 1m 55cm. She often wears high-heeled shoes!
h Yes, she is.
i She was composing songs at the age of just 13.

2 Make a quiz about a celebrity from TV, movies, music, or sports.
Follow the steps in the project checklist.

> ## ○ PROJECT CHECKLIST
>
> **1** Choose your celebrity.
> **2** Find out about him / her using magazines or the Internet.
> **3** Write 8–10 questions about him / her. Think about his / her life, achievements, and ideas. Organize your questions under headings. Make sure you have the answers to your questions!
> **4** Make a quiz with your texts and pictures. Write your answers on a different piece of paper.

3 Exchange your quiz with the rest of the class. Who knows the most about your celebrity?
Then give them the answers and ask them to match them with your questions.
How fast can they do it?

6

Life in numbers

Start thinking

1 How many years are there in a millennium?
2 Do you have a lucky number? Why is it lucky?
3 What's your personality like?

Aims

Communication: I can ...

• use a wide variety of numbers and times.
• understand a text about numbers.
• make predictions using *will* and *won't*.
• talk about people's personality.
• talk about conditions and their results.
• speak about the future.
• write a report about a survey.

Vocabulary

• Time and numbers
• Adjectives: characteristics

Language focus

• *will, won't*
• First conditional
• Expressing probability
• *nobody* and *everybody*

Reach Out Options

Extra listening and speaking

Can I take a message?

⇨ Page 93

Curriculum extra

Math: Statistics and charts

⇨ Page 101

Culture

The U.S. in numbers

⇨ Page 109

Vocabulary puzzles

Time and numbers; Adjectives: characteristics

⇨ Page 117

VOCABULARY ◼ Time and numbers
I can use a wide variety of numbers and times.

1 ● 2.29 Complete the lists with the words in the box. Then listen and check.

> a billion   a century   a couple   a day   a half
> zero   a second   a thousand   a year

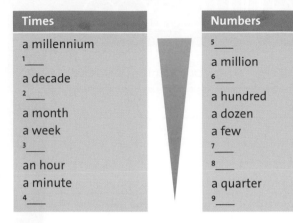

Times
a millennium
1 ____
a decade
2 ____
a month
a week
3 ____
an hour
a minute
4 ____

Numbers
5 ____
a million
6 ____
a hundred
a dozen
a few
7 ____
8 ____
a quarter
9 ____

2 ● 2.30 Listen and say the numbers.

Numbers	0.2	1,965	2,800	
Ordinals	fifth	twelfth	thirteenth	twentieth
Dates	1965	2008		
Prices	$6.40	$12.50		
Distances	100 kilometers			

3 Correct the sentences using numbers and ordinals.

1 There are **third** bedrooms in our house. ✗
2 Elizabeth Blackwell was the **one** woman to become a doctor. ✗
3 I live on the **twelve** floor of an apartment building. ✗
4 She finished **two** in the race. ✗
5 My dad traveled to other countries **fifth** times last year. ✗

4 ● 2.31 Work in pairs. Do the *Numbers quiz* on page 59. Then listen and check your answers.

5 **ACTIVATE** Work in pairs. Ask and answer the questions.

1 What's your date of birth?
2 What's your lucky number?
3 What's your house or apartment number?
4 In what year will you be twenty?
5 What's the price of a movie ticket in your town?
6 How long do you need to sleep each night?
7 How much money do you need to be happy?

○ *Finished?*
Write five more questions for the *Numbers quiz*.
What is the population of the U.S.?
a 160 million   b 211 million   c 313 million   d 404 million

Numbers

QUIZ

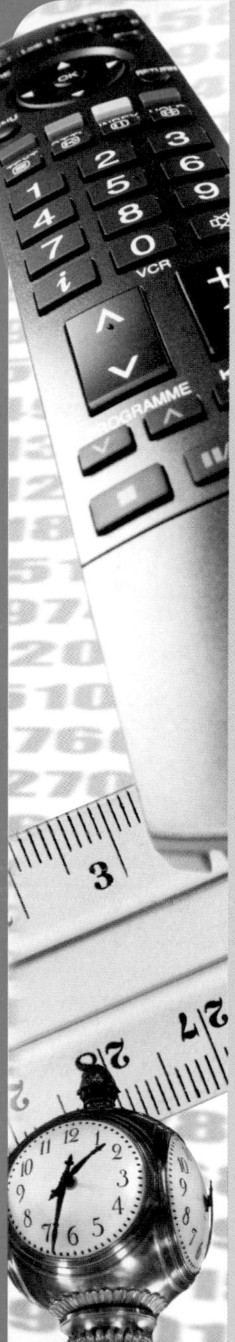

1 What is the average life of a human in years?
a 77   b 88   c 66   d 99

2 What is the approximate population of the planet?
a 4 billion   b 4 million   c 7 million   d 7 billion

3 What is the distance from London to New York?
a 585 kilometers   b 1,585 kilometers
c 5,585 kilometers   d 10,585 kilometers

4 How many millimeters are there in a kilometer?
a 100,000   b 10,000,000
c 1,000,000   d 100,000,000

5 How many years are there in a millennium?
a 1,000   b 100   c 10   d 1,000,000

6 What is half of a dozen?
a four   b five   c six   d seven

7 How much time does the average child in the U.S. watch TV every day?
a 1 hour   b 2 hours   c 3 hours   d 5 hours

8 In which century was William Shakespeare born?
a 15th   b 16th   c 17th   d 18th

9 What distance is a marathon running race?
a 22.519 kilometers   b 32.915 kilometers
c 42.195 kilometers   d 52.591 kilometers

10 How many minutes are there in three quarters of an hour?
a 30   b 40   c 45   d 60

11 What was the year of the first Olympic Games?
a 776 BC   b 136 BC   c AD 1844   d AD 2004

12 What is the number pi (π)?
a 1.621   b 3.142   c 2.118   d 9.876

NEW YORK
5304 KM

TREPASSEY
3941 KM

PARIS
575 KM

LONDON
291 KM

1 Look at the picture of the buttons in the elevator. What do you notice? Why do you think this happens?

2 ● 2.32 Read the text. Add sentences a–e to the paragraphs. There is one sentence that you do not need. Then listen and check.

   a Maybe he'll change the number to 12½!

   b So a building whose top floor is 50 may only have 36 floors.

   c In 2016, a lot of children will be eight years old in China!

   d Seven is a lucky number in most cultures.

   e Eight is also a popular number in phone numbers, addresses, and PIN numbers.

3 **BUILD YOUR VOCABULARY** Check the meaning of the words in blue in the text. Then complete the sentences.

   1 She's happy, healthy, and rich. She's ___.

   2 Many people have a ___ of the dark.

   3 My aunt doesn't like black cats. She's very ___.

   4 I never win anything. I'm ___.

   5 I think the number 13 is unlucky. It's my ___.

4 **ABOUT YOU** Ask and answer the questions.

   1 Are you superstitious about any numbers?

   2 What superstitions can bring you good or bad fortune?

   3 Do you have a fear of anything?

   4 Do you have a lucky number?

   5 Do you think you are a lucky person or an unlucky person? Why?

Lucky numbers

At eight minutes past eight on the eighth day of the eighth month of 2008, the Olympic Games started in Beijing. In China, eight is a lucky number, and people believe that an eight in your date of birth will bring good fortune. Millions of Chinese people tried to have an "Olympic baby", and in 2008, there were a lot more births than in a normal year. **1**___

But why eight? In Mandarin, the pronunciation for eight (*ba*) sounds similar to the word for "prosperity." In 1992, someone paid $640,000 for a license plate with the single number 8 on it. **2**___

In contrast, you won't be lucky in China if you have the number four in your date of birth. The number four in Mandarin (*si*) sounds like the word for "death," so many people think it is an unlucky number, which will bring you bad fortune. In many East Asian countries, buildings don't have any floor numbers with a four in them. **3**___

In some European countries and in the U.S., the unlucky number is thirteen. The superstition started because Judas was the thirteenth person at the Last Supper. People with a fear of the number thirteen are triskaidekaphobic. Unfortunately, the phobia can also affect people who aren't superstitious, like the man who was happy to buy house number 13 on his street, but couldn't sell it. **4**___

LANGUAGE FOCUS ◼ *will, won't*
I can make predictions using *will* and *won't*.

1 Complete the sentences from the text on page 60. Then complete the rules.

People believe that an eight in your date of birth **will** bring good fortune.

In 2016 a lot of children ¹___ be eight years old in China!

You ²___ be lucky in China if you have the number four in your date of birth.

◯ RULE

We use ___ / ___ + base form when we make a prediction about the future.

2 Match the questions with the answers. Then complete the rules.

1 Will 2044 be a lucky year in China?
2 What will an eight in your date of birth bring you?
3 Will a lot of children be eight years old in China in August 2016?

a Good fortune.   b Yes, they will.
c No, it won't.

◯ RULES

1 We make questions with ___ + subject + base form.
2 We make short answers with *Yes,* / *No,* + pronoun + *will* / ___.

(More practice ⇨ Workbook page 49)

3 Write sentences. Predict the future for you and your friends.

Eva will write a book.

1 write a book   4 become a teacher
2 visit China   5 be on TV
3 buy a fast car   6 travel a lot

4 Study the key phrases. Then use them to compare your predictions in exercise 3 with a partner.

KEY PHRASES ◯ Making predictions

I think (that) … .   I imagine (that) … .
I bet (that) … .   I'm pretty sure (that) … .

(I think that Eva will write a book.)

(Pronunciation: *'ll* ⇨ Workbook page 91)

5 Make predictions with the words in the boxes, and *will* and *won't*. Compare your predictions with your partner using the key phrases.

| People | • go to school
• live on other planets
• be more intelligent
• speak one language | • in the next few years.
• in the next century.
• in the next millennium. |
| The world | • be a better place
• be a desert
• exist
• be cleaner | • soon.
• in the future.
• one day. |

(People won't be more intelligent in the future.)

(Really? I'm pretty sure they will be more intelligent.)

6 Order the words to make questions.

will / where / you / live / when you're older
Where will you live when you're older?
1 have / how many / children / you / will
2 you / be a millionaire / will
3 will / do / job / what / you
4 be alive / will / you / in the next century
5 you / when / will / leave home

STUDY STRATEGY ◯ Speaking clearly

7 Read instructions 1–3.

1 Read the question before you speak.
2 Practice saying the question quietly. Memorize it.
3 Look at your partner when you speak.

8 ACTIVATE Ask and answer questions about your future with a partner. Use the questions in exercise 6 or your own ideas. Use the study strategy.

◯ *Finished?*
Imagine the world 50 years from now. Write predictions using *will* and *won't*.
Children won't study in schools.

1 Work in pairs. Write pairs of opposite adjectives using one adjective from box A and one from box B.

> A ~~helpful~~ easygoing impatient ambitious friendly negative shy generous creative modest peaceful serious

> B stingy patient outgoing moody positive unambitious unfriendly funny ~~unhelpful~~ arrogant aggressive unimaginative

helpful – unhelpful

2 Choose adjectives from box A to describe the people.

Adam is very relaxed. **easygoing**

1 Ben always gets the best grades on tests, but he never talks about it.
2 Katie always does the dishes.
3 Simon always gives us expensive presents.
4 Jenny wants to be the best at everything.
5 Tom is a quiet and calm boy.
6 Rachel always thinks everything is bad.
7 Josh doesn't like big parties.
8 Sally is good at meeting new people.
9 Mark hates waiting.
10 Ellie writes stories and songs.
11 Tim doesn't like having fun.

NUMEROLOGY:
numbers and personality

Add the digits in your birth date until you have a number between 1 and 9.

Examples:
Johnny Depp – 06/09/1963
= 6 + 9 + 1 + 9 + 6 + 3 = 34 = 3 + 4 = 7
Jennifer Aniston – 02/11/1969
= 2 + 1 + 1 + 1 + 9 + 6 + 9 = 29 = 2 + 9 = 11 = 1 + 1 = 2

3 Look at the *Numerology* test and calculate the number for someone in your family.

> My brother's number is 6. I agree that he is sometimes impatient!

4 🔘 2.33 Listen to Holly, Mark, and Becky, and answer the questions.

1 Who doesn't believe in numerology at all?
2 Who thinks horoscopes are fun?
3 Who thinks these tests can really describe your personality?

5 🔘 2.33 Listen again and complete the sentences with one or two words.

1 Mark's birthday is ___.
2 Mark and Holly were born in the year ___.
3 The test says Mark is creative, generous, and ___.
4 Becky's numerology number is ___.
5 Becky says she isn't ___.

6 **ACTIVATE** Look at the *Numerology* test and calculate your number. Do you agree? Explain your answers.

It's true because I'm creative. I like writing stories. I'm also sometimes moody, especially in the morning!

1	+	positive, likes action
	−	sometimes aggressive
2	+	modest, thinks about other people
	−	sometimes shy
3	+	artistic, has a good imagination
	−	sometimes negative
4	+	practical, likes organizing
	−	sometimes serious
5	+	positive, likes doing things
	−	sometimes impatient
6	+	artistic, likes helping people
	−	sometimes impatient
7	+	intelligent, peaceful
	−	sometimes argues
8	+	works a lot, good at deciding things
	−	sometimes ambitious, occasionally impatient
9	+	creative, generous
	−	sometimes moody

LANGUAGE FOCUS ■ **First conditional**
I can talk about conditions and their results.

1 Choose the correct words in the sentences you heard in the listening on page 62. Then complete the rules with *condition* and *result*.

If you ¹ **go** / **'ll go** to a café today, you ² **meet** / **'ll meet** two friendly girls.

We ³ **find out** / **'ll find out** if you ⁴ **tell** / **'ll tell** me your birthday.

⁵ **Do** / **Will** you leave me alone if I ⁶ **tell** / **'ll tell** you?

○ RULES

1 We use the first conditional to talk about a condition in the future and the result of this condition.
2 We describe the ___ with *if* + simple present.
3 We describe the ___ with *will* + base form.
4 The sentence can start with the ___ or the result.
5 We never use *If* + *will*: ~~If you will go, I'll be happy.~~ ✗

(More practice ⇨ Workbook page 51)

2 Choose the correct words.

SUPERSTITIONS FROM AROUND THE WORLD

1 If it rains when someone moves to a new house, they **'re** / **'ll be** rich. (Iceland)

2 If you **'re** / **'ll be** the seventh son of a seventh son, you'll have special powers. (Ireland)

3 You **won't** / **don't** get married if you sit at the corner of a table. (Russia)

4 Your money will disappear if you **put** / **will put** your wallet on the floor. (Brazil)

5 If you **see** / **will see** a spider in your house, people **visit** / **will visit** you. (Turkey)

6 You'll **lose** / **lose** your memory if you **wash** / **'ll wash** your hair on the day of a test. (Korea)

3 Complete the text using the first conditional. Who is the person you will meet?

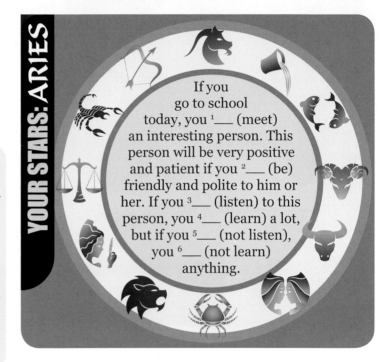

YOUR STARS: ARIES

If you go to school today, you ¹___ (meet) an interesting person. This person will be very positive and patient if you ²___ (be) friendly and polite to him or her. If you ³___ (listen) to this person, you ⁴___ (learn) a lot, but if you ⁵___ (not listen), you ⁶___ (not learn) anything.

4 Complete the sentences with your own ideas. Use the first conditional.

1 Our teacher will be happy … .
2 If I become rich and famous, … .
3 What will we do …?
4 He's shy. If you talk to him, … .
5 If it's sunny this weekend, … .

5 **ACTIVATE** Work in pairs. Ask and answer first conditional questions using the words in the table and your own ideas.

		do	your homework early tonight?
		buy	
		go	your keys?
What		see	a lot of money?
Where	(not)	meet	the movies tonight?
Who		remember	shopping?
		finish	the park later?
		lose	

What will you do if you finish your homework early tonight?

If I finish it early, I'll go out and meet some friends.

○ *Finished?*
What horoscope sign is your partner? Invent a horoscope prediction for him or her.

Allison	Caleb, can I ask you some questions? I'm doing a survey.
Caleb	Yes, sure, Allison.
Allison	Right, the first question is, "Do you think that the world will be a better place in the future?"
Caleb	Let me think ... No, definitely not. I think it'll be a worse place.
Allison	Why's that?
Caleb	Because I think we won't have enough energy. What about you?
Allison	I disagree with you.
Caleb	What do you think, then?
Allison	I think it'll probably be a better place because we'll invent other forms of energy.
Caleb	OK. What's the next question?
Allison	The next question is ... .

1 Look at the picture. What are Caleb and Allison doing?

2 ● 2.34 Listen and read the dialogue. Are Caleb and Allison positive or negative about the future?

3 Find the key phrases in the dialogue. Who says them?

> **KEY PHRASES ○ Asking for and giving opinions**
>
> 1 What about you?
> 2 I agree / disagree with you.
> 3 I think it'll ... .
> 4 Why's that?
> 5 Do you think ... ?
> 6 Let me think.

Language point: Expressing probability

4 Study the answers to the question, *Do you think that the world will be a better place in the future?* Order the answers. Start with the most probable.

> No, probably not.   Yes, probably.
> Yes, definitely.   No, definitely not.

1 Yes, definitely.   2 __   3 __   4 __

5 Study the example sentences. Where do we put *probably* and *definitely* in affirmative and negative sentences?

It'll probably be a better place.
I probably won't go.
They'll definitely help us.
They definitely won't understand.

(More practice ⇨ Workbook page 51)

6 Look at the *Future survey*. Write answers for questions 1–6 using *probably (not)* and *definitely (not)*, and your reasons.

I think that the world will probably be a better place in the future because we won't have as many problems.

7 **ACTIVATE** Look again at the dialogue in exercise 2. Change the words in blue and practice a new dialogue using the *Future survey*. Extend your dialogue to include questions 2–6 from the *Future survey*.

```
FUTURE SURVEY
Human life in the future

1 Will the world be a better place in
  the future? Why / Why not?
2 Will humans become more intelligent?
3 Will humans become more friendly?
4 Will space travel be normal in the
  next hundred years?
5 Will humans live on other planets in
  the future?
6 Will you travel into space if you
  have the opportunity?
```

WRITING ■ **A report on a survey**
I can write a report about a survey.

6

REPORT: The next millennium survey

The topic of the survey was "Human life in the future." A group of ten people did the survey and in general they were positive about the future. These are the results:

More than half of the group think that the world will be a better place in the future. Some people think that the world will be better because we will learn to protect the planet. A lot of people think that humans will become more intelligent, but nobody thinks that we will become more friendly.

Most people think that space travel will be normal in the next century and about half of the people think that humans will live on other planets in the future. Everybody says that they will travel into space if they have the chance.

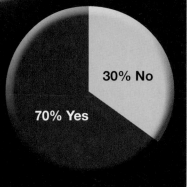

Will the world be a better place in the future?

30% No
70% Yes

1 Read the model text and answer the questions.

1 How many people did the survey?
2 How many people think the world will be a better place?
3 Where do about half the people think that humans will live?
4 Is the language formal or informal?

2 Order the phrases. Start with the phrase which expresses the smallest quantity.

KEY PHRASES ○ Expressing quantity

more than half	nobody
one or two people	half
most / a lot	some
everybody	

Language point: *nobody* and *everybody*

3 Study the survey. Then choose the correct words. Do we use a singular or plural verb with *nobody* and *everybody*?

A superstition survey

	Yes	No
Do you have a lucky number?	8	2
Do you read horoscopes?	7	3
Are you superstitious?	3	7
Do you stay at home on the 13th day of the month?	0	10

1 **Most / Half** of the group have a lucky number.
2 **A lot of / One or two** people read horoscopes.
3 **More than half / Some** are superstitious.
4 **Everybody / Nobody** stays at home on the 13th day of the month.

4 **ACTIVATE** Follow the steps in the writing guide.

○ WRITING GUIDE

A TASK

Do a class survey about the future. Write a report with the results.

B THINK AND PLAN

Look again at the *Future survey* on page 64. Answer the questions as a class. Complete the table and use the information in your report.

Results of the *Future survey*		
	Yes	No
Question 1 ... Question 2 ...		

C WRITE

Paragraph 1: Introduction
Topic and general opinion: question 1
Paragraph 2:
People in the future: questions 2–3
Paragraph 3:
Travel in the future: questions 4–6

D CHECK

• singular and plural verbs
• quantity expressions
• *nobody* and *everybody*

Vocabulary

1 Complete the phrases with the words in the box.

> billion   couple   decade   dozen   quarter

1 a ___ of an hour = 15 minutes
2 a ___ = two
3 a ___ = twelve
4 a ___ = 10 years
5 a ___ = a thousand million

2 Find pairs of opposite adjectives.

1 funny   a unimaginative
2 moody   b aggressive
3 peaceful   c easygoing
4 patient   d serious
5 creative   e impatient

Language focus

3 Complete the questions and answers with the pairs of verbs in the box. Use *will*.

> take / go   have / not get   have / start
> go / study

1 "___ your brother ___ to college?"
  "Yes, he will. I think he ___ English."
2 "What time ___ you ___ dinner this evening?"
  "I imagine that Dad ___ cooking at half past six, so at about seven o'clock."
3 "___ you ___ children when you're older?"
  "No, I won't. And I ___ married."
4 "Where ___ you ___ the dog for a walk?"
  "I think I ___ to the park."

4 Choose the correct form of the verbs to make conditional sentences.

1 If you **put** / **will put** your keys in your bag, you **don't** / **won't** lose them.
2 You **don't** / **won't** forget his birthday if you **write** / **will write** it in your diary.
3 If you **go** / **will go** shopping on Saturday, **will** / **do** you buy Sam a birthday present?
4 If you **don't** / **won't** buy a ticket soon, there **aren't** / **won't** be any left.
5 I **call** / **'ll call** you later if I **remember** / **will remember**.

5 Match 1–5 with a–f. Then write first conditional sentences. There is one ending you do not need.

1 you are unfriendly
2 you take out the trash
3 they forget my birthday
4 it's a scary movie
5 you not have any money

a we do the dishes
b I play soccer
c people not speak to you
d I be really upset
e I buy you a drink
f I not watch it

Communication

6 Complete the dialogue with the phrases in the box.

> me think   I'm pretty   I imagine
> think that   do you   why's that
> I agree   what about you

Jenny ¹___ think that we will use books in the future?
Mark   Let ²___. ³___ sure that we won't use normal books.
Jenny ⁴___?
Mark   Well, computers will be cheaper and lighter. ⁵___ that we'll all have small electronic books for everything. ⁶___?
Jenny ⁷___ with you. I ⁸___ we'll use them for everything – reading and writing.
Mark   I can't wait. Books are heavy!

Listening

7 ● 2.35 Listen to Zoe and her dad. Then choose the correct answers.

1 This evening, Zoe wants to …
  a go to the movies.   b go to a party.
  c stay at home.
2 The party will finish at …
  a 10:00 p.m.   b 10:30 p.m.   c 11:00 p.m.
3 Zoe and her dad agree that she will leave at …
  a 10:00 p.m.   b 10:30 p.m.   c 11:00 p.m.
4 What will Zoe's dad do if Zoe isn't outside at the right time?
  a He'll drive home.
  b He'll talk to Zoe's mom.
  c He'll go into the party.

Listening

1 Look at the pictures and complete the words.

1 c___

2 w___

3 p___

4 c___

5 p___

6 s___

2 ● 2.36 Listen to Alan, Bess, and Lily talking about future plans. Which job in exercise 1 do they **not** mention?

3 ● 2.36 Listen again and complete the sentences with one or two words.

1 Bess went to bed ___ than usual.
2 Bess's ___, David, has a "life plan."
3 If David gets good grades in ___, he'll be a programmer.
4 David is more ___ Bess.
5 Bess thinks she'll be a ___ before she gets married.
6 Lily thinks she'll become a ___ or a ___.
7 Alan thinks he'll become a ___.
8 Bess doesn't think that Alan can ___.

Speaking

4 What will you do after you leave school? Think about what you enjoy now and make predictions about your future. Answer the questions.

1 Will you go to college?
2 What job will you do?
3 Will you learn to drive?
4 Where will you live?
5 When will you leave home?
6 Will you get married?

5 Work in pairs and have a conversation. Use your ideas in exercise 4 and the chart below to help you. One of you is A and one of you is B. When you finish, change roles.

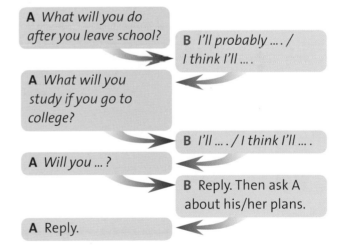

A *What will you do after you leave school?*

B *I'll probably .... / I think I'll ... .*

A *What will you study if you go to college?*

B *I'll ... . / I think I'll ... .*

A *Will you ... ?*

B *Reply. Then ask A about his/her plans.*

A *Reply.*

Writing

6 Write ten ideas for your own "life plan." You can write about the plans you talked about in exercise 5 or you can describe new plans.

If I go to college, I'll ... .

7

Sports for all

Start thinking

1 Which sports do you like? Why?
2 Are there sports events for disabled people?
3 What companies sponsor sports teams?

Aims

Communication: I can ...

- make suggestions about sports.
- understand an interview.
- talk about plans and predictions.
- talk about sports.
- talk about future arrangements.
- invite a friend to a sports event.
- write a letter to ask for sponsors.

Vocabulary

- People in sports
- Compound nouns: sports

Language focus

- Imperatives
- *be going to*
- *will* and *be going to*
- *be going to*: questions
- Present continuous for future arrangements
- Indefinite pronouns
- Layout and language in a formal letter

Reach Out Options

Extra listening and speaking
Talking about scores
⇨ Page 94

Curriculum extra
Math:
Average speed
⇨ Page 102

Culture
National sports
⇨ Page 110

Vocabulary puzzles
People in sports;
Compound nouns: sports
⇨ Page 118

VOCABULARY ■ People in sports

I can make suggestions about sports.

1 ● 3.02 Match photos 1–6 with six of the words in the box. Then listen and check.

> captain   champion   finalist   supporter   TV reporter
> manager   owner   referee   sponsor   loser   coach

2 Complete the sentences with your own ideas.

1 ___ is the captain of ___.
2 ___ is the manager of ___.
3 ___ were champions last year.
4 ___ were finalists in a big competition last year.
5 ___ are sponsors of ___.

3 Work in pairs. Play the *Team manager* game on page 69.

Language point: Imperatives

4 Study the imperative sentences in the table. Then answer the questions.

Affirmative	Negative
Buy the player.	Don't buy the player.
Speak to them.	Don't speak to them.

1 What is the difference between the affirmative and negative forms?
2 Do you use a subject with the imperative?

> More practice ⇨ Workbook page 57

5 **ACTIVATE** Work in pairs. A friend wants to become an athlete. Make suggestions. Use affirmative and negative imperative forms of the words in the box.

> contact   drink   eat   go out late   go to bed
> practice   plan   smoke

Practice every day.

○ *Finished?*
Think of some good and bad situations for a team manager. Use the words in exercise 1.
Good – your sponsors want to give your team more money.

TEAM MANAGER

> ➤ **You're the manager of a team.**
> ➤ **Look at the situations and make decisions.**
> ➤ **Then look at the key.**

The captain of the team is very negative at the moment.
a Change the captain.
b That's OK. He's a good player.

You have the best coach in the world. He wants to go to another team, but he has a contract with your club.
a He must stay. He has a contract.
b He must go if he isn't happy.

The owner of the club wants to buy a player. The player isn't very good, but he's the owner's friend.
a Buy the player.
b Don't buy the player.

You think that a referee made very bad decisions in a game.
a Speak to journalists and players about the referee.
b Don't speak to journalists or players about the referee.

The sponsors want to change the name of the club.
a Accept. You need the money.
b Don't accept. The club and its name are 100 years old.

OXTOWN UNITED

PGI ELECTRONICS

You were champions last year. Now you can buy new players.
a Don't buy new players. Your team is good.
b Buy new players. The team can always be better.

$30,000,000

Some journalists say that you're a loser and you aren't a good manager.
a Don't speak to them.
b Be patient and polite.

Sport — World's worst manager?

The supporters aren't coming because the tickets are too expensive.
a Don't change the price. Play better.
b Change the price and play better.

KEY

MOSTLY a: Watch out! You aren't a bad person, but as a manager you are sometimes negative. You must also learn to be more flexible.

MOSTLY b: Congratulations! You're a good manager. You're fair and very positive. You're flexible, but you also have principles.

Driving Ambition

Karen Lowe wants to be the fastest woman on four wheels.

A My dad used to race cars, and I watched him when I was younger. I loved the crowds and the atmosphere. I competed in karts when I was nine. Then I drove rally cars. I really like Formula 3. This year, I'm going to give it a shot.

B It's massive! The U.K. is a world center for auto racing. There are 750 clubs in this country and 100,000 competitors.

C Not at all. There are more women competitors than you think, but you don't see them very often because there aren't a lot of women in Formula 1.

D Not many women were interested in the past. Also, journalists, sponsors, and some drivers didn't support us. Now they say that it's good to have more women in the sport. I think the situation will change.

E Yes, there will be a woman champion, one day. Definitely.

F Not at all! Racing is really hard. Obviously, you have to be a great driver. Apart from that, you need a lot of money in this sport. Last year, I was OK, but this year, my sponsors aren't going to give me much money. I think I'll be OK, but I can never be certain.

G I'm not going to stop racing! My dad is my manager now and he's going to contact more sponsors. I know that my family will always support me. They're my biggest supporters.

1 Male athletes are often more famous than female athletes. Why is this? Is it fair? Is this situation changing? How?

2 ● 3.03 Read the interview and match interview questions 1–6 with answers A–G in the text. Then listen and check.

Are most of the competitors men?   *C*
1 How popular is auto racing in the U.K.?
2 How did you become interested in racing?
3 So, what are your plans?
4 Why are there fewer women in Formula 1?
5 Is it easy to become a racing champion?
6 Will a woman win Formula 1 one day?

3 Read the text again and complete the sentences with one, two, or three words.
1 Karen ___ her dad when she was a girl.
2 After karts, Karen raced ___.
3 Auto racing is ___ in the U.K.
4 In the future, more women will become ___.
5 Karen doesn't have a lot of ___ this year.
6 Her dad needs to find more ___ this year.

4 **BUILD YOUR VOCABULARY** Complete the sentences with the words in blue in the text.
1 Which soccer team do you ___?
2 I don't know how to play hockey, but I want to ___.
3 She ___ in the championship. She won!
4 My brother loves motorcycle ___.
5 The ___ was pretty serious. He broke his leg.
6 The crowd cheered. The ___ was amazing.

5 **ABOUT YOU** Ask and answer the questions.
1 What kind of racing do you like?
2 What team sports do you compete in?
3 Which sports do you want to try?
4 Which teams do you support?
5 Who are your favorite sports stars?

LANGUAGE FOCUS ■ *be going to* • *will* and *be going to*
I can talk about plans and predictions.

7

be going to

1 Order the words to make sentences. Check your answers in the text on page 70. Then choose the correct words in the rule.

1 going to / I'm / give it a shot / this year
2 racing / stop / going to / I'm / not
3 contact / he's / going to / more sponsors
4 going to / me much money / aren't / my sponsors / give

○ RULE

We use *be going to* to **make predictions / explain plans and intentions**.

More practice ⟹ Workbook page 57

2 Study the information and complete the sentences.

Plans	Karen	Karen's dad
Find more sponsors	✗	✓
Buy a new car	✓	✓
Race next year	✓	✗
Contact journalists	✗	✓
Look for a manager	✗	✗

Karen's dad **is going to find** more sponsors.
1 Karen and her dad ___ a new car.
2 Karen ___ next year.
3 Her dad ___ next year.
4 Her dad ___ journalists.
5 Karen ___ journalists.
6 They ___ a manager.

3 Write sentences about your plans using the affirmative and negative form of *be going to*. Then talk about your plans with a partner.

(join) a tennis club next year
1 (race) motorcycles when I'm older
2 (support) a different soccer team next season
3 (go) to the Olympics when I'm older
4 (watch) sports on TV this weekend
5 (play) basketball soon
6 (give) basketball a shot one day

I'm not going to join a tennis club next year.

will and *be going to*

4 Study the examples. Which sentence is a plan and which is a prediction?

1 This year I'm going to give Formula 3 a shot.
2 I think the situation will change.

More practice ⟹ Workbook page 57

5 Write sentences with *be going to* (for plans and intentions) or *will* (for predictions).

I think that our team **will win**. (win)
1 The players ___ tomorrow morning. (meet)
2 That was great! Your manager ___ very happy with you. (be)
3 The finalists ___ at three o'clock. (play)
4 Maybe you ___ a journalist when you're older. (be)
5 Her coach ___ next month. She told me yesterday. (leave)

STUDY STRATEGY ○ Remembering grammar

6 Read the study strategy. Then write examples of two plans and two predictions. Memorize them. Then tell your plans and predictions to a partner without looking at your work.

1 When you learn a new grammar rule, write example sentences in your notebook.
2 Memorize your sentences and test yourself every week.

7 ACTIVATE Write sentences about your plans and predictions. Use the ideas in the box and your own ideas. Then discuss with a partner.

My predictions	My plans
win the league	one day
be a champion	today
finish this book	this year
have a Ferrari	when I'm older

○ Finished?
Write three predictions and three plans or intentions for next year.

1 🔘 3.04 **Choose the correct words. Then listen and check.**

1 Wimbledon is a famous British **tennis tournament / tennis instructor**.
2 Australia won the last **rugby game / rugby player**.
3 Chelsea is my favorite **soccer fan / soccer team**.
4 Michael Phelps is an American **swimming race / swimming champion**.
5 The new **track and field champion / track and field stadium** holds 20,000 people.
6 Maracanã is a good **team manager / soccer stadium**.

2 **Work in pairs. Complete the sentences with a word from box A and a word from box B.**

> A soccer tennis basketball
>   track and field bike baseball skiing

> B tournament champion competition
>   player stadium team race

The Champions League is a *soccer tournament*.
1 Usain Bolt is a ___.
2 The Tour de France is a ___.
3 Turner Field is a ___.
4 A grand slalom is a ___.
5 The Chicago Bulls are a ___.
6 Rafael Nadal is a ___.

3 🔘 3.05 **Look at the pictures and listen to three interviews about disabled people and sports. Which person is from Hawaii?**

4 🔘 3.05 **Write *true* or *false*. Then listen again and correct the false sentences.**

1 Susan is going to prepare for one skiing competition next year.
2 Susan is going to talk to children about sports.
3 A shark attacked Bethany Hamilton in 2003.
4 Bethany is going to compete in New York next month.
5 Harriet's basketball team is going to buy a new bus.
6 The basketball team is going to play a game in New York on Friday.

5 **ACTIVATE Write six more quiz questions using compound nouns from exercise 2. Then ask and answer your questions with a partner.**

1 When does the soccer tournament start?
2 How many people are on a basketball team?

Harriet

Susan

Bethany

LANGUAGE FOCUS ■ *be going to*: questions • Present continuous for future arrangements
I can talk about future arrangements.

be going to: questions

1 Complete the questions from the interviews on page 72 with the words in the box.

> going to   how   is   is   what   where

1 ___ are you going to do next season?
2 ___ are you going to go?
3 Are you ___ be one of the ski instructors?
4 ___ she going to keep competing? Yes, she ___.
5 ___ are you going to spend the prize money?

(More practice ⇨ Workbook page 59)

2 Order the words to make questions.

1 going to / play / are / you / tennis / later
2 going to / join / you and your friends / any teams / next year / are
3 go / to any tournaments / you / going to / are / this year
4 your friend / going to / is / go bike riding / this weekend
5 going to / what sport / you / are / play / next week

3 Work in pairs. Ask and answer the questions in exercise 2.

Present continuous for future arrangements

4 Study mini-dialogues a and b. Then match them with rules 1 and 2.

a "Do you have any plans for the weekend?"
"Yes, I'm meeting my friend on Sunday."
"Are you meeting her in the gym?"
"No, we're meeting in the park."

b "Hi! What are you doing?"
"I'm watching a game on TV right now."

◯ RULES

1 We can use the present continuous when we talk about arrangements in the future. We often use a time expression when we talk about future arrangements.

2 We also use the present continuous when we talk about actions in progress. (See page 21)

(More practice ⇨ Workbook page 59)

5 Study the sentences. Then write *action in progress* or *future arrangement*.

When are you going to the movies?
future arrangement

Hi. Are you waiting here for Steven?
action in progress

1 Where are you having dinner tonight?
2 Sorry, are you talking to me?
3 I'm meeting Tom on Sunday morning.

6 Complete the mini-dialogues using the present continuous form of the verbs in the box.

> ride   do   practice   swim   visit   watch

1 "What's happening on Monday afternoon?"
"We ___ for the running race."
2 "Do you have any plans for the summer vacation?"
"Yes, we ___ across the U.S. on our bikes."
3 "What are you up to this weekend?"
"I ___ my cousins in Denver!"
4 "___ you ___ anything on Saturday?"
"Yes, I ___ at the local pool. There's a big competition."
5 "Do you want to come to the café tomorrow?"
"I can't. I ___ my dad play rugby."

7 ACTIVATE Work in pairs. Ask and answer the questions in blue in exercise 6. Use the present continuous for future arrangements and your own ideas.

(What's happening on Monday afternoon?)

(I'm meeting Sara. We're playing soccer.)

(Pronunciation: Recognizing contractions ⇨ Workbook page 92)

◯ *Finished?*

Write six sentences about imaginary future arrangements.

I'm meeting Roger Federer on Saturday afternoon.

Lydia	Seth ... Seth!
Seth	Yes? Oh, hi, Lydia.
Lydia	¹___
Seth	²___ Why? ³___
Lydia	I'm going to a basketball game ⁴___
Seth	Yes, great. What time does it start?
Lydia	⁵___ eight o'clock at the community center.
Seth	OK. Is anyone from school going?
Lydia	No, but someone you like is going to be there!
Seth	Who?
Lydia	Lucy!
Seth	Oh, OK. ⁶___ the community center at about seven thirty.
Lydia	Yeah, OK. I'll see you there.
Seth	See you later, Lydia.

1 ● 3.06 Listen and read the dialogue. Where and when are Seth and Lydia meeting?

2 ● 3.06 Study the key phrases. Who says each phrase? Listen and check.

> **KEY PHRASES ○ Making plans**
>
> a What are you up to?
> b Are you doing anything this evening?
> c ... if you're interested.
> d No, nothing special.
> e Let's meet outside ....
> f It starts at ...

3 ● 3.06 Complete the dialogue with the key phrases. Listen again and check. Then practice the dialogue with a partner.

Language point: Indefinite pronouns

4 Study the examples. When do we use *any-* and *some-*?

Is anyone from school going?

Someone you like will be there.

There isn't anywhere to play tennis.

5 Complete the sentences with the indefinite pronouns in the box.

> anything   anyone   somewhere   something

1 Is ___ from school going to the game?
2 There's a tennis court ___ in the park.
3 There isn't ___ to watch on TV.
4 There's ___ I want to tell you.

(More practice ⇨ Workbook page 59)

6 **ACTIVATE** Imagine that you want to invite a friend to a tennis tournament or a soccer game. Look at the posters and choose one. Invent a dialogue. Change the words in blue in the model dialogue. Practice your dialogue with a partner.

WRITING ● A formal letter
I can write a letter to ask for sponsors.

7

1 Read the model text and answer the questions.

1 What is the letter writer's name?
2 Do we know the name of the person who is going to receive the letter?
3 Which paragraph gives a suggestion about what to do next?
4 Which paragraph explains the event?
5 Which paragraph introduces the writer and explains what she needs?

Language point: Layout and language in a formal letter

2 Study the text again and answer the questions.

1 Where is the writer's address?
2 Where is the date?
3 Where is the address of the company that is going to receive the letter?
4 Does the writer use full forms of verbs or contractions? Find examples.
5 Does the writer use formal or informal phrases? Find examples.

3 Study the key phrases. Then order them.

> **KEY PHRASES ○ Writing formal letters**
>
> ___ I am writing to you because … .
> ___ Yours faithfully,
> ___ Please contact me … .
> ___ I look forward to hearing from you.
> 1 Dear Sir or Madam,

SALEM

BOUNCERS

190 Lions Street, Salem, Oregon 97301

Creditbank Limited
1650 First Street
Portland, Oregon 97312

May 3

Dear Sir or Madam,

Ⓐ I am the captain of a basketball team in Salem. The team's name is the Salem Bouncers. I am writing to you because we are planning a tournament and we are looking for sponsors.

Ⓑ The tournament will take place in Salem in August. Teams and fans from six states are going to be in Salem for this event. Sponsoring this event will be good publicity for your company.

Ⓒ Please contact me if you are interested in sponsoring us or if you need further information. I look forward to hearing from you.

Yours faithfully,

Mary Grant

Mary Grant (Team Captain)

4 ACTIVATE Follow the steps in the writing guide.

> ## ○ WRITING GUIDE
>
> ### A TASK
>
> You are going to compete in a bike riding competition. Write a formal letter to a local company about becoming your sponsor.
>
> ### B THINK AND PLAN
>
> Read the model text again. Then order ideas a–e for your new letter.
> a Need a sponsor
> b Planning to compete in a big competition
> c Member of the Cyclox bike riding team
> d Teams from 23 states
> e In Boston in May
>
> ### C WRITE
>
> **Paragraph 1: Introduction**
> Who are you? Why are you writing?
> **Paragraph 2: Explain the event**
> Give information about the competition.
> **Paragraph 3: Suggest what to do next**
> Ask the person to contact you.
>
> ### D CHECK
>
> • layout of the letter
> • formal expressions
> • full form of verbs (not contractions)

Vocabulary

1 Find the odd one out in each group.

1 captain   finalist   coach   trophy
2 bike race   supporter
   tennis tournament   basketball game
3 rugby team   manager   owner   referee
4 journalist   TV reporter   ski season
   sponsor

2 Choose the correct words.

> I usually watch my team's soccer
> ¹ **games / sponsors / situations** on the TV.
> TV is OK, but the ² **atmosphere / season /
> trophy** inside a big soccer ³ **court / race /
> stadium** is much more exciting. On TV, it's
> often difficult to see the ball, but at a real
> game, you can see and hear everything. The
> ⁴ **journalists / referees / supporters** sing
> their team's songs and they shout at the
> other team's players. They also shout when
> they disagree with the ⁵ **owner's / coach's /
> referee's** decisions!

Language focus

3 Give advice to the new girl on the running
team (number 5). Write affirmative and
negative imperative sentences using the words
in the boxes.

> arrive   eat   listen   run   wear

> chocolate   late for races   running shoes
> the coach   every day

4 Write sentences using *be going to* or *will*.

1 I think / my favorite team / win / the
   national championship next year
2 who / win / the game tomorrow / ?
3 I / go / to the movies / with Nick / later
4 they / not play / tennis tomorrow. They're
   going to play soccer.
5 the P.E. teacher / talk to / us tonight

5 Complete the sentences using the present
continuous for future arrangements form of
the verbs.

1 We ___ to the game on Saturday. (not go)
2 ___ the captain tonight? (the owner / meet)
3 They ___ the tennis tournament at 5:00.
   (watch)
4 I ___ on Saturday. I'm playing basketball. (not
   swim)
5 You ___ in the next race. (not compete)
6 ___ on the team tomorrow? (you / play)

Communication

6 Complete the letter with the words in the box.

> contact   faithfully   forward   madam
> sir   writing

> Dear ¹___ or ²___,
> I am ³___ to you because I love tennis.
> Are you looking for people to work at
> the tournament next month? I am very
> interested in working for you. I can work
> every weekend.
> Please ⁴___ me at 503-555-9560.
> I look ⁵___ to hearing from you.
> Yours ⁶___,
> Roger McEnroe

Listening

7 ● 3.07 Listen to the telephone conversation.
Then complete the sentences with one, two, or
three words.

1 When Ben calls, Mel is ___.
2 L.A. Galaxy is a ___ team.
3 L.A. Galaxy has a new ___.
4 They ___ 2:30 p.m.
5 Ben ___ buy the tickets online.

1 Read the proposal. What's your opinion of Ethan's solutions?

Proposals for sports in Peoria by Ethan King

I live in Peoria. We have $100,000 to improve the sports facilities. If we spend it on the right things, this city will be much better for everyone. What do you think of my proposals?

Swimming facilities

There is a successful swim team in Peoria, but the city swimming pool is dirty and old. If we build a new swimming pool, it will definitely use all of the money.
Proposal: The council should find business sponsors. If they give 50% of the money, then we'll build a swimming pool and still have money for other projects.

Now give your opinion.

Making sports affordable

There aren't many sports facilities in Peoria. There's a modern leisure center 6 km away, but not many young people use it. It's difficult to get there if you can't drive and it also has lots of sports that people don't know about, such as taekwondo and trampolining.
Proposal: They should start a bus service to the sports center, with a bus pass for younger people. If the sports center organizes short courses over the summer vacation, people can give new sports a shot.

Now give your opinion.

Improving the local youth center

There aren't many things for young people in Peoria, but there's a youth club. It's a good place because a lot of people come here, especially in winter, but the rooms are dirty and boring. There's lots of space outside, but nobody uses it.
Proposal: They should use the outside space for a basketball court and a skatepark. If there is something good outside, there will be more visitors in the summer.

Now give your opinion.

☺ Good idea!
😐 I'm not sure.
☹ Bad idea!

2 Make a proposal for sports facilities in your neighborhood or city. Follow the steps in the project checklist.

⚪ PROJECT CHECKLIST

1 Think of three things that you'd like to change. What will be better if the changes are made?

2 Take a picture of each thing that you're writing about, or find one on the Internet or in a magazine.

3 Write a short introduction to your neighborhood or city. Then write a paragraph for each of the three things. Describe the situation at the moment, say why you'd like to change it, and make a proposal.

4 Make a poster with your texts and pictures. Include an opinions key, so that other students can give their opinion of your proposals.

3 Exchange your proposal with the rest of the class. What's your opinion of their proposals?

Are you scared?

Start thinking

1 What's a roller coaster? Is it fun or scary?
2 What is arachnophobia?
3 What's the most dangerous job in the world?

Aims

Communication: I can ...

- explain how I feel about activities.
- talk about fears and phobias.
- talk about experiences.
- talk about injuries I've had.
- ask about people's experiences and react to their answers.
- help someone with an injury.
- describe an accident.

Vocabulary

- Feelings
- Injuries

Language focus

- Modifiers
- Present perfect: affirmative and negative
- Present perfect: questions
- *so* and *because*

Reach Out Options

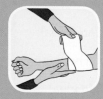

Extra listening and speaking

Calling a medical helpline

⇨ Page 95

Curriculum extra

Language and literature: Stories

⇨ Page 103

Culture

The police

⇨ Page 111

Vocabulary puzzles

Feelings; Injuries

⇨ Page 119

VOCABULARY ▪ Feelings

I can explain how I feel about activities.

1 Do the *Risks and danger* questionnaire. Then look at the key. Do you agree?

2 Add *about*, *at*, *in*, or *of* to each adjective. Then check your answers in the questionnaire on page 79.

enthusiastic **about**

1 bad	3 good	5 interested	7 scared
2 fond	4 happy	6 worried	8 stressed out

3 Are the phrases in exercise 2 positive or negative?

Language point: Modifiers

4 Complete the table with the modifiers in blue in the questionnaire. Do the modifiers go before or after the adjective?

Weak feeling				Strong feeling
←				→
1___	not very	2___	really	3___

5 Choose the correct words.

1 I like motorcycles and I'm **pretty interested in / not at all happy about** motorcycle racing.
2 I like trying new dishes. I'm **very worried about / really fond of** curries and spicy food.
3 Alan's **really enthusiastic about / pretty worried about** skateboarding. He skateboards every day!
4 I'm **not at all happy about / pretty fond of** swimming in deep water. It's really scary!
5 I'm **not very scared of / really bad at** cooking. My pasta dishes are terrible!
6 Sue's **very enthusiastic about / not very fond of** mountain biking. She goes mountain biking every Sunday.

(More practice ⇨ Workbook page 65)

6 **ACTIVATE** Work in groups. Ask and answer questions about the activities in orange in exercise 5. Use modifiers and adjectives.

> I'm really interested in motorcycle racing. What about you?

> No, I'm not at all interested in racing.

> ⬤ *Finished?*
> **Write five questions using the phrases in exercise 2.**
> *Are you scared of spiders?*

Risks and danger

How adventurous are you?

1 Thrills

a I love scary roller coasters. I'm not worried about anything. I'll try anything once.

b I'll try things if they aren't too scary, but I'm frightened of things that are high or fast.

c I hate roller coasters! I prefer to have my feet on the ground.

2 Martial arts and adventure sports

a I like martial arts and I've tried one of these sports: climbing, mountain biking, or skiing.

b I've often wanted to try climbing or skiing.

c I'm not at all enthusiastic about martial arts or adventure sports.

3 New experiences

a I'm very fond of exotic food, especially Chinese and Indian food.

b I've tried one or two new dishes this year.

c I'm not good at eating spicy food, like curry.

4 In the wild

a I like being outside in a storm in the dark. It's great!

b I'm not very enthusiastic about being outside in a storm.

c I never go out in a storm and I don't like the dark.

5 Phobias

a I'm really interested in insects. I've had spiders and insects on my hand. I'm not scared of them.

b I've touched a spider or insect, but I wasn't happy about it!

c I'm scared of spiders and insects. I don't go near them.

6 Speaking in public

a I often speak in English in front of my class. I'm not really scared of speaking in public.

b I've spoken English in front of my class, but it isn't fun. I get pretty stressed out about it.

c I never speak in front of the class in any language. I'm bad at speaking in public.

KEY

Mostly a: You love risks and danger! You're definitely adventurous, but be careful. Life isn't just a game.

Mostly b: You aren't scared of danger and you enjoy adventure, but you don't take unnecessary risks.

Mostly c: It's good to respect danger, but a life without risks is boring. Why not try an adventure sport or some exotic food? You might discover a new "you."

Feel the fear!

I hate spiders. A lot of people dislike spiders, but I'm really scared of them. If there's a spider in a room, I won't go in. I have stayed at friends' houses three times because there were spiders in our house. It sounds ridiculous, but if you don't have a phobia, you won't understand. I do have a phobia – arachnophobia.

Two months ago, I went with my mom to see a specialist named Mark Tanner. Mark has helped a lot of patients with phobias. Some patients had "normal" phobias, like being frightened of dogs, or snakes, or the dark. Some patients had really weird ones, like phobias of bananas, or eating in public. He's helped a girl with a phobia of school as well. She hasn't been at school this year!

I've seen the specialist a few times and he's been really helpful. First, we looked at pictures of spiders, and then we watched spiders on a DVD. Next, he gave plastic spiders to my family and they hid them around the house. That was really unpleasant, but it's made me much less phobic. I also wrote in my "spider diary" every time I saw a real spider.

I've looked at hundreds of spiders with Mark and my phobia has improved a little. That's the idea of "exposure therapy." After you've seen a thousand spiders, you aren't scared of them anymore. Next week, Mark says that I must touch one. I don't think I'm ready for that! I haven't touched a spider before and I don't know if I can. We'll see …

by Georgia Bushell, Cleveland, Ohio

Some phobias and their names

fear of flying – aerophobia
fear of thunderstorms – brontophobia
fear of being in a small space – claustrophobia
fear of dentists – dentophobia
fear of teenagers – ephebiphobia
fear of snakes – ophidiophobia

1 **Answer the questions.**

1 What are you scared of?
2 Do you have any phobias?
3 What is the difference between a fear and a phobia?

2 ● 3.11 **Read and listen to the text. How can you cure a phobia?**

3 **Read the text again and write *true* or *false*. Correct the false sentences.**

1 There were spiders at Georgia's house.
2 Georgia was Mark Tanner's first patient.
3 Some people are scared of eating in public.
4 Georgia's family hid real spiders at home.
5 Georgia is less scared of spiders now.
6 Georgia is definitely going to touch a spider.

4 **BUILD YOUR VOCABULARY Find adjectives 1–5 in blue in the text. Then match them with definitions a–f. There is one definition you do not need.**

1 ridiculous	a having a phobia
2 weird	b existing, not imaginary
3 unpleasant	c being scared of spiders
4 phobic	d very silly, absurd
5 real	e not nice
	f unusual, strange

5 **ABOUT YOU Ask and answer the questions.**

1 What do you think of spiders and insects?
2 What do you think is unpleasant?
3 Is it ridiculous to be scared of flying?
4 Are you scared of anything that isn't real? What?

LANGUAGE FOCUS ■ Present perfect: affirmative and negative
I can talk about experiences.

8

1 Complete the sentences from the text on page 80. Then choose the correct answers in the rules.

1 He ___ a girl with a phobia of school.
2 I ___ the specialist a few times.
3 It ___ me much less phobic.
4 After you ___ a thousand spiders ....

○ RULES

1 We use the present perfect to talk about experiences in the **past / present** which are important **now / in the future**.
2 We **say / don't say** exactly when a present perfect action happened.
3 We form the present perfect with *have / be* + past participle.
4 We often use the short forms: *'ve, 's.*

More practice ⟹ Workbook page 65

STUDY STRATEGY ○ Checking and learning past participles

2 Complete the table with the simple past and past participle forms of the verbs in the box.

~~do~~ speak find go ~~help~~ look
see make play stay touch visit

Simple past and past participle forms	
regular	**irregular**
help – helped – helped	do – did – done

3 Work in pairs. Cover your tables and test your partner. What are the simple past and past participle forms of the verbs in exercise 2?

4 Complete the sentences using the present perfect form of the verbs.

The specialist *has helped* Georgia. (help)
1 I ___ Mark Tanner a few times. (see)
2 They ___ about their phobias. (not speak)
3 You ___ at her house. (not stay)
4 We ___ at a lot of spiders. (look)
5 Georgia ___ a spider before. (not touch)

5 Complete the text using the present perfect form of the verbs in the box.

go have not find not speak see
upset visit

School phobia

Peter Ford [1]___ to school only three times in three months. He [2]___ two different specialists, but they [3]___ a solution to his problem. Peter is terrified of school, but he [4]___ to many people about his problems. The police [5]___ Peter's parents because it's illegal not to go to school.

In the U.S., about 4.7% of school-aged children have a phobia of school, or *didaskaleinophobia*. A lot of them are scared of school because they are worried about being away from home. This sometimes happens because something [6]___ them in their life, like moving, changing schools, or because they [7]___ problems with friends or family.

6 **ACTIVATE** Work in pairs. Talk about experiences 1–8. Use the words in the box and the affirmative and negative forms of the present perfect.

Everyone My friends I My mom / dad
Nobody One of my friends
One or two people in my class

1 see a shark
2 visit the U.S.
3 save $200
4 drive a car
5 win a competition
6 have a pet insect
7 study English
8 live in another country

One of my friends has seen a shark.

○ *Finished?*
Write six ridiculous sentences about experiences.
I've met President Obama!
I haven't done any homework this year!

1 Check the meaning of the words. Then complete the table.

Verb	Past participle and / or adjective	Noun
cut	cut	a cut
burn	¹___	a burn
²___	broken	a break
bruise	bruised	³___
⁴___	bitten	a bite
sprain	sprained	⁵___
injure	⁶___	an injury

2 Choose the correct words.

1 He's been in the sun and he's **burned** / **injured** his nose.
2 I fell off my bike. I have some **cuts and bruises** / **breaks and bites**.
3 Ouch! That mosquito has **injured** / **bitten** me!
4 One of their best players is **injured** / **injury**.
5 I've never **break** / **broken** my leg.
6 How did you **cut** / **bruised** your hand?

3 Look at pictures A–D and match them with jobs 1–4 in the program guide.

4 ● 3.12 Work in pairs. Write *true* or *false*. Then listen and check your answers. Correct the false sentences.

1 Volcanologists know a lot about volcanoes.
2 Volcanoes erupt quite frequently.
3 Venomologists study dangerous places.
4 Fishing is the most dangerous job.
5 Farming is dangerous because of the weather.

5 ● 3.12 Listen again and complete the sentences with one, two, or three words.

1 Leo Williams has visited four places in ___.
2 When the volcano erupted, Ted Amber had a ___ and some burns.
3 Snakes ___ Sasha a few times.
4 Dan Murphy has ___ toe and ___ his arms this season.
5 Jill Brown works ___ farm.
6 ___ cause accidents to farmers.

6 **ACTIVATE** Work in pairs. Talk about injuries you have had. Use the words in exercise 1 and the words in the box.

> arm   foot   hand   head   leg   nose

> I've broken my leg.

DANGER AT WORK!

Preview: Leo Williams speaks about his new documentary series. Leo has traveled around the U.S., talking to people with dangerous jobs.

Sasha Jacobs ¹Venomologist   **Dan Murphy** ³Fisherman
Ted Amber ²Volcanologist   **Jill Brown** ⁴Farmer

LANGUAGE FOCUS ■ Present perfect: questions
I can ask about people's experiences and react to their answers.

1 Complete the sentences with the words in the box. Then choose the correct words in the rule.

> ever   has   ~~has~~   have   no   they

1 ~~Has~~ he traveled around the U.S.?
  Yes, he ___.
2 Has a snake ___ bitten you?
  ___, it hasn't.
3 ___ they had many accidents?
  Yes, ___ have.

○ **RULE**

We make present perfect questions by using *Have / Has* + subject + (ever) + **infinitive / past participle** + other words.

More practice ⇨ Workbook page 67

2 Choose the correct words.

1 **Have / Has** you bruised your leg?
  Yes, I **have / has**.
2 Has Tim **had / have** an accident?
  No, he **haven't / hasn't**.
3 **Have / Has** the train arrived?
  Yes, it **have / has**.
4 **Has / Have** they visited Montana?
  No, they **hasn't / haven't**.
5 Have you **broken / break** your arm?
  No, I **haven't / hasn't**.

3 Write questions and answers. Use the information in the table.

	Bess Kline (stunt person)	Vin Hardman (bodyguard)
(break) a bone	✔	✘
(jump) off a building	✔	✘
(meet) the president	✘	✔
(drive) at 200 km/h	✔	✔

Bess (break)
Has Bess broken a bone? Yes, she has.
1 Vin (break)
2 Bess (jump)
3 Bess (meet)
4 Vin (meet)
5 they (drive)

4 Write questions using *ever* and the present perfect form of the verbs.

(do) a stunt?
Have you ever done a stunt?
1 (touch) a spider?
2 (swim) across a river?
3 (break) a bone?
4 (meet) a famous person?
5 (visit) a volcano?
6 (have) a spider bite?

Pronunciation: /ɪ/ and /i/ ⇨ Workbook page 92

5 ● 3.13 Complete the key phrases with the words in the box. Then listen and check.

> amazing   have   haven't   neither

KEY PHRASES ○ Reacting
Really?
I have! ¹___ you?   That's ³___ !
So ²___ I!   ⁴___ have I.

6 ACTIVATE Work in pairs. Ask and answer the questions in exercise 4 using the key phrases.

> Have you ever done a stunt?

> No, I haven't.   Neither have I.

○ *Finished?*
Invent jobs for your friends. Write about their experiences.
Stefan is a volcanologist. He's traveled to Hawaii.

SPEAKING ● Helping with problems
I can help someone with an injury.

Teacher	Leah, what's wrong? Are you OK?
Leah	I've ¹hurt my arm.
Teacher	Have you broken it?
Leah	No, I've ²cut it.
Teacher	How did that happen?
Leah	It was an accident. ³I fell while I was running to the basketball game.
Teacher	Oh, right. Have you ⁴cleaned it?
Leah	Yes, I have, but it hurts.
Teacher	Do you need help?
Leah	⁵No, I think I'll be OK.
Teacher	Maybe you need to ⁶see a nurse.

1 ● 3.14 **Look at the picture. What has happened? Listen to the dialogue and check. Then practice the dialogue with a partner.**

2 Match key phrases 1–4 with a–d.

> **KEY PHRASES ○ Helping someone**
>
> 1 What's wrong? a rest your leg.
> 2 Are you OK? b I think I've sprained my ankle.
> 3 How did that happen? c I was playing soccer in the gym.
> 4 Maybe you need to ... d Yes, I think so.

3 Match pictures 1–8 with the words in the box.

> ankle elbow finger knee neck
> shoulder toe wrist

4 Work in pairs. Ask and answer questions using the key phrases.

1 elbow? (bruise) 4 finger? (break)
2 toe? (cut) 5 knee? (injure)
3 shoulder? (burn) 6 ankle? (sprain)

> **What's wrong with your elbow? Are you OK?**

> **No, I think I've bruised it.**

5 **ACTIVATE** Replace the phrases in blue in the dialogue with phrases a–f. Write and practice a new dialogue with your partner.

a hurt my finger d go to the drugstore
b put it in cold water e I put my hand on the stove.
c No, it isn't serious. f burned it

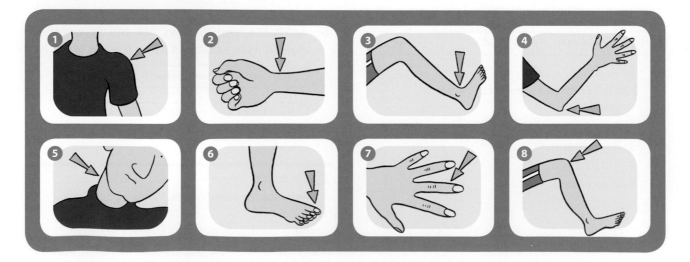

WRITING ■ E-mails
I can describe an accident.

A Hiya Kate,

Thanks for your last e-mail. How's it going? Have you heard from Amy?

Guess what! I've broken my leg! **B** It happened last Saturday when I was walking in the mountains with Nick. **C** It was getting dark, so we were hurrying. Suddenly, I fell down. I landed on a rock about three meters down the side of the mountain. **D** I couldn't move my legs, so Nick called the rescue services. They arrived really quickly. I went to hospital in their helicopter!

E I'm really bored now because I'm still in the hospital. I've been in bed for three weeks! I've read three books, so that's good. Write back soon.

See you,

Jen

1 Read the e-mail and find three examples of the present perfect and three examples of the past continuous.

2 Match descriptions 1–5 with parts of the e-mail A–E.

1 What she was doing when the accident happened. **C**
2 Greetings and introduction.
3 Where and when the accident happened.
4 What's happened since the rescue.
5 What happened as a result of the accident.

3 Match key phrases 1–5 with meanings a–f. There is one meaning that you do not need.

KEY PHRASES ○ Writing e-mails

1	How's it going?	a	Has (Amy) written / spoken to you?
2	Have you heard from (Amy)?	b	I miss you.
3	Guess what!	c	How are you?
4	Write back soon.	d	Listen to my news!
5	See you	e	Send me an e-mail.
		f	Goodbye

Language point: *so* and *because*

4 Complete the examples and rules with *so* or *because*.

1 I'm really bored now ___ I'm still in the hospital.
2 It was getting dark, ___ we were hurrying.

○ RULES

1 We use ___ to give a reason.
2 We use ___ to explain a result.
3 We use a comma before ___, but not before ___.

5 ACTIVATE Follow the steps in the writing guide.

○ WRITING GUIDE

A TASK

Imagine that you had an accident while you were playing soccer or basketball. Write an e-mail to a friend.

B THINK AND PLAN

Check the meaning of the words. In what order will you put the words in your e-mail?

ambulance   fall over   broken ankle
score a goal / a basket   kick / throw   hospital

C WRITE

1 Greetings and introduction.
2 Where the accident happened.
3 What you were doing when the accident happened.
4 The result of the accident.
5 What's happened since the accident.

D CHECK

• informal phrases
• *because* and *so*
• use of present perfect and past tenses

Vocabulary

1 Choose the correct words.

1 "I'm not **interested / bad / fond** in horror movies."
"Neither am I. They're usually **worried / phobic / ridiculous**."

2 "Are you **phobic / good / interested** about anything?"
"Yes, I'm **scared / bad / good** of dogs!"

3 "Is she **worried / stressed out / fond** of spiders?"
"No, she thinks they're really **unpleasant / phobic / real**."

4 "What are you **bad / worried / good** about?"
"My best friend sent me a **weird / fond / scared** text message."

5 "Math is a **real / worried / phobic** problem for me."
"Me too. I'm really **fond / interested / bad** at it."

2 Complete the words.

1 Something has bi_ _ _ _ my foot.
2 Is that a bru_ _ _ on your arm?
3 Has Kim sp_ _ _ _ _ _ her wrist?
4 He fell and in_ _ _ _ _ his leg.
5 I've bu_ _ _ _ my hand.
6 He has some c_ _ _ on his face.
7 When did you bre_ _ your arm?
8 That's a bad in_ _ _ _. Will she be OK?

Language focus

3 Choose the correct words.

1 I'm **not at all / pretty / very** enthusiastic about roller coasters. They're horrible and scary!

2 I love cake and I'm **not very / not at all / really** fond of chocolate cake.

3 My doctor **isn't very / is very / is really** worried about me. He says I'll be OK soon.

4 I'm **pretty / really / not at all** interested in movies. I sometimes go to the movie theater, but not often.

5 She's **pretty / very / not very** good at running. She won all the races last year.

6 You're **not at all / really / not very** stressed out about something. What's wrong?

4 Complete the sentences using the present perfect form of the verbs.

1 You don't know Lee. You ___ him. (not meet)
2 He loves scary places. He ___ a few volcanoes! (visit)
3 We'll be late. Our bus ___. (not arrive)
4 I'm quite good at basketball. I ___ for our school in three important finals. (compete)
5 It's my first Spanish class today. I ___ Spanish before. (not study)

5 Look at the picture. Write present perfect questions and short answers.

1 the man / break / his foot
2 the girls / sprain / their ankles
3 the mother / cut / her leg
4 the mother / hurt / her arm
5 the boys / burn / their arms
6 the man / bruise / his arm

Communication

6 Complete the dialogue.

Amy What's ¹w_ _ _g?
Lisa I think I've ²b_ _ _ _n my finger.
Amy How did that ³h_ _ _ _n?
Lisa It was an ⁴a_ _ _ _ _ _t.
Amy Are you OK?
Lisa Yes, I ⁵t_ _ _k so.
Amy Maybe you ⁶n_ _d to go to the hospital.

Listening

7 ⊙ 3.15 Listen to Luke and Sara talking about their jobs and complete the table.

	Luke	Sara
Job	Diving instructor	³___
Feeling about job	¹___	⁴___
Injury	²___	⁵___

Listening

1 〔● 3.16〕 Listen to the conversation. Then answer the questions.

1 What is Lily doing?
   a She's reading a magazine.
   b She's writing a questionnaire.
   c She's doing her homework.
2 What is the questionnaire about?
   a surfing
   b being brave
   c phobias

2 〔● 3.16〕 Look at pictures A–F. In what order do they appear in the conversation? Listen again and check.

3 〔● 3.16〕 Listen again and complete the sentences with one or two words.

1 Alan thinks he is ___ person at school.
2 Alan isn't ___ spiders.
3 Bess and Alan have never touched ___.
4 Alan is ___ sharks.
5 Bess loves ___.
6 Alan doesn't like doing ___.

Speaking

4 Write the questions from Lily's questionnaire and prepare three more questions using the present perfect and *ever*. Use the words in the boxes and your own ideas.

> be   climb   dive   drive   jump   see
> swim   touch   watch   ride

> bridge   elephant   horror movie
> mountain   plane   mountain bike
> roller coaster   shark   snake   spider

5 Work in groups of three. Take turns to ask the questions from exercise 4. Use the chart below to help you. Who is the bravest in your group?

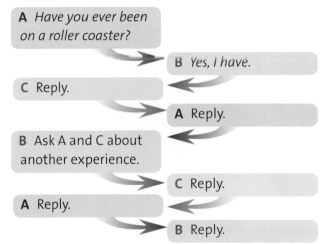

A *Have you ever been on a roller coaster?*
B *Yes, I have.*
C Reply.
A Reply.
B Ask A and C about another experience.
C Reply.
A Reply.
B Reply.

Writing

6 Write about two true experiences and one false experience. Write twenty words about each experience. Read your experiences to a partner. Can your partner guess the false experience?

I've ... .
It happened when ... .

EXTRA LISTENING AND SPEAKING ■ Joining a club
I can ask for and give personal information.

1

1 ● 1.11 Match parts of an application form 1–7 with information a–g. Then listen and check.

1 date of birth   5 postal address
2 e-mail address   6 zip code
3 first name   7 last name
4 cell phone number

a   Mark
b   Haywood
c   mark.haywood@webwise.com
d   773-210-1077
e   June 25, 1997
f   7254 West Adams Street
g   60617

2 ● 1.12 Look at the pictures and match them with the words in the box. Then listen to a conversation between an assistant at a youth club and Eve. What class does Eve join?

> drama   horseback riding   judo
> scuba diving

3 ● 1.12 Study the key phrases. Then listen to the conversation again and answer the questions.

> **KEY PHRASES ○ Asking for and giving personal information**
>
> I'd like to join ... .
> How do you spell your last name?
> Can I have your contact details?
> My e-mail address is ... .
> It's $ ... for a year's membership, please.

1 What is Eve's last name?
2 What is Eve's cell phone number?
3 What city does Eve live in?
4 What time does the first drama class start?
5 What costs $45?

4 ● 1.13 Listen and repeat the dialogue.

Mark   Hello. I'd like to join the scuba diving club.
Clerk   Of course. No problem. What's your date of birth?
Mark   It's June 25, 1997.
Clerk   Great. What's your name?
Mark   Mark Haywood.
Clerk   How do you spell your last name?
Mark   It's H–A–Y–W–O–O–D.
Clerk   Can I have your contact details?
Mark   Yes. My e-mail address is mark.haywood@webwise.com. My cell phone is 773-210-1077.

5 Copy the application form in exercise 1. Complete it with your personal information.

6 ACTIVATE Change the words in blue in the dialogue in exercise 4 using the information in your application form. Then practice your new dialogue with a partner.

Reach Out Options

EXTRA LISTENING AND SPEAKING ● Finding things
I can talk about the location of things.

2

1 ● 1.26 **Listen to eight false sentences about the picture. Correct the sentences using the prepositions in the box.**

> behind between on in in front of
> ~~near~~ next to under

1 The microwave is in front of the sink.
   The microwave is near the sink.

2 ● 1.27 **Listen to Ava and her dad. What are they looking for?**

3 ● 1.27 **Study the key phrases. Then listen to the conversation again and answer the questions.**

> **KEY PHRASES ○ Finding things**
>
> Look, here's … !
> Is this what you're looking for?
> That's the wrong one.
> Here it is!

1 Why does Ava need the book today?
2 Where are Ava and her dad?
3 Where does she usually do her homework?
4 Where does Ava find the book?
5 Why does she want to find her brother?

4 ● 1.28 **Look at the house plan and listen. Then practice the dialogue with a partner.**

Stacey What's wrong?
Danny I can't find my laptop.
Stacey Is it under the table in the living room?
Danny No, it isn't.
Stacey Look, here's a laptop! Is this what you're looking for?
Danny No, that's the wrong one.
Stacey What about the bedroom? Is it next to the dresser?
Danny No, it isn't. Oh, here it is! It's on the bed.

5 ACTIVATE **Change the words in blue in the dialogue in exercise 4 using the information in the house plan. Then practice your new dialogue with your partner.**

EXTRA LISTENING AND SPEAKING ■ An event in the past

I can talk about an event in the past.

3

1 🔘 1.39 **Listen to people talking about a party. Match speakers 1–4 with the topics they are talking about, a–e. There is one topic that you do not need.**

a people   **d** food
b music   **e** presents
c drinks

1 Sara
2 Tom
3 Kate
4 James

2 🔘 1.40 **Listen to Sophia talking about a party. Which of the things in the box does she talk about?**

> drinks   Sally's parents   music
> games   food

3 🔘 1.40 **Study the key phrases. Then listen to the conversation again and answer the questions.**

> **KEY PHRASES ⭕ Talking about an event**
>
> Why didn't you go to …?
> How was it?
> I had a great time.
> Were there many people?
> What was the music like?
> What did you buy him / her for a present?

1 Where was Karen on the night of Sally's party?
2 Who was at the party?
3 What is Ruth (Sally's sister) like?
4 Who played the music?
5 What did Sophia buy Sally for a present?

4 🔘 1.41 **Listen to the dialogue. Then practice it with a partner.**

Rob   Hi, Sam. Why didn't you go to Jack's birthday party?

Sam   I couldn't come. It was my dad's birthday and we went out to a restaurant. How was it?

Rob   Fantastic! I had a great time!

Sam   Were there many people?

Rob   Yes, there were about 100 people. I met Jack's sister, Rebecca. She's cool.

Sam   I don't know her. What was the music like?

Rob   Really good. And there were lots of snacks and drinks.

Sam   What did you buy him for a present?

Rob   I bought him a computer game. He really liked it!

5 **ACTIVATE Change the words in blue in the dialogue in exercise 4 using the information in the diary. Then practice your new dialogue with your partner.**

> I went to Chloe's birthday party on Saturday. Emma couldn't go. She was at her grandfather's house. He lives about 100 km away.
>
> I thought the party was amazing. About 50 people were there. I met Chloe's brother, Mark. He was really friendly. The music was really good and Chloe's cousins made lots of great snacks. I bought Chloe a poster and she loved it!

EXTRA LISTENING AND SPEAKING ● Directions
I can ask for and give directions.

4

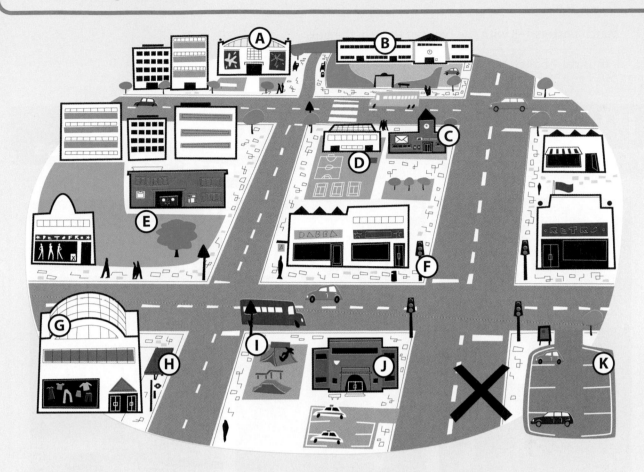

1 🔘 2.10 **Match words 1–11 with the words in the box to form compound nouns. Then listen and check.**

> mall center club ~~gallery~~ lot park
> office light school station stop

1 art **gallery**
2 bus ___
3 parking ___
4 police ___
5 post ___
6 middle ___
7 shopping ___
8 skateboard ___
9 sports ___
10 traffic ___
11 youth ___

2 **Look at the map and match places A–K with the words in exercise 1.**

A art gallery
B m___ s___
C p___ o___
D s___ c___
E y___ c___
F t___ l___
G s___ m___
H b___ s___
I s___ p___
J p___ s___
K p___ l___

3 🔘 2.11 **Study the key phrases. Then listen. Where do the people want to go? Start at "X."**

> **KEY PHRASES ⭕ Asking for and giving directions**
> Do you know where the (youth club) is?
> How do I get there?
> Turn left / right at (the traffic light).
> It's on the left / right.
> Go straight ahead.

4 🔘 2.12 **Listen. Then practice the dialogue.**

Liam	Excuse me. Do you know where the youth club is?
Police officer	Yes, it isn't far.
Liam	How do I get there?
Police officer	Turn left at the traffic light. Then go straight ahead. Cross the road. The youth club is on the right.
Liam	Great! Thanks for your help.
Police officer	You're welcome.

5 **ACTIVATE Change the words in blue in exercise 4. Then practice your new dialogue with your partner. Use the map.**

Reach Out Options

EXTRA LISTENING AND SPEAKING ● **Buying tickets**
I can buy tickets for a play or movie.

5

1 Match posters 1–3 with the types of show in the box.

> musical   ballet   play

PHOENIX THEATER

AUTUMN PROGRAM

TICKETS: $23, $28, $35

①
Swan Lake
Tchaikovsky
September 1–30

②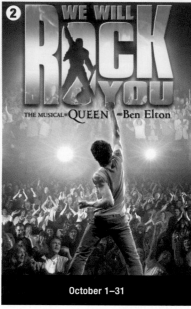
WE WILL ROCK YOU
THE MUSICAL BY QUEEN AND Ben Elton
October 1–31

③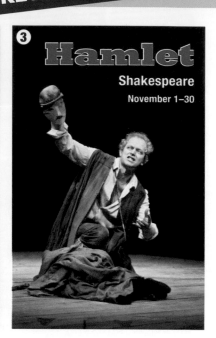
Hamlet
Shakespeare
November 1–30

2 🔘 2.23 Look at the posters and listen to the conversation. Which type of show is Tom buying tickets for?

3 🔘 2.23 Study the key phrases. Then listen to the conversation again. Complete the ticket with the correct information.

> **KEY PHRASES ◯ Buying tickets**
>
> Can I have two tickets for ..., please?
> Where would you like to sit? Front, middle, or back?
> That's seats ... and ... in row ... .
> That's $ ... altogether, please.

TICKET

Show:	¹___
Date:	October ²___
Seats:	³___ ⁴___
Row:	⁵___
Total price:	⁶___

THEATER

4 🔘 2.24 Listen and write the numbers and letters. Then listen and repeat.

5 🔘 2.25 Listen to the dialogue. Then practice the dialogue with a partner.

Amy   Can I have three tickets for Swan Lake, please?
Clerk   Certainly. Which date?
Amy   September 22.
Clerk   Where would you like to sit? Front, middle, or back?
Amy   Front, please.
Clerk   Certainly. That's seats 41, 42, and 43 in row B. They're $35 each.
Amy   Great!
Clerk   That's $105 altogether, please.
Amy   Here you are.
Clerk   Thanks. Enjoy the show.

6 ACTIVATE Change the words in blue in exercise 5 using the information in the posters. Then practice your new dialogue with your partner.

EXTRA LISTENING AND SPEAKING ● Can I take a message?

I can leave a phone message for someone.

6

1 Match types of information 1–5 with details a–e.

1	phone number	a	68 Long Street
2	time	b	18:40
3	date	c	212-555-1498
4	price	d	August 18
5	address	e	$9.50

2 ● 2.37 **Listen and write the details. Then listen again and repeat.**

3 ● 2.38 **Listen to a telephone conversation and a message. Which numbers from exercise 1 do you hear?**

4 ● 2.38 **Study the key phrases. Then listen to the telephone conversation and message again and answer the questions.**

> **KEY PHRASES ○ Leaving a message**
>
> Can I speak to ... , please?
> He's / She's out at the moment.
> Can I take a message?
> Can you ask him / her to call me?
> Can you tell him / her that ... ?

1 Where is Logan when Lucy phones?
2 What message does Logan's dad take?
3 Where are Lucy and Logan going this evening?
4 What will happen if Logan is late?

5 ● 2.39 **Read the message and listen to the dialogue. Then practice the dialogue with a partner.**

> *Matt, Steven called. He's meeting the girls at eight o'clock tonight at the movie theater.*

Matt's mom	Hello.
Steven	Hi, it's Steven here. Can I speak to Matt, please?
Matt's mom	Sorry, he's out right now. Can I take a message?
Steven	Yes, please. Can you tell him that I'm meeting the girls at eight o'clock at the movie theater?
Matt's mom	OK, meeting the girls ... eight o'clock ... movie theater.
Steven	That's right.
Matt's mom	OK, I'll give him the message.
Steven	Thanks. Bye.
Matt's mom	Bye.

6 ACTIVATE **Change the words in blue in exercise 5 using the information in the messages. Then practice your new dialogue with your partner.**

> *Matt, Rachel called. She's having a party on Saturday, September 16 – 53 First Street.*

> *Matt, Craig called. The tickets for the concert cost $12.95.*

EXTRA LISTENING AND SPEAKING ● Talking about scores

I can talk about the scores in soccer games.

1 Check the meaning of the words in the box. Then complete the sentences with the words.

fan goal game score

1 Paula is a big Liverpool ___.
2 He's going to ___! Yes!
3 What a beautiful ___!
4 Do you want to watch the ___ on TV?

2 ● 3.08 **Listen to the conversation. Which game are Paula and Andy watching?**

3 ● 3.08 **Study the key phrases. Then listen to the conversation again and write** *true* **or** *false*. **Correct the false sentences.**

> **KEY PHRASES** ◯ **Talking about sports**
>
> What's the score?
> It's 3–3 (three all).
> It's 1–0 (one–nothing) for … .
> I think it'll be a draw.
> I'm sure we'll win / lose.

1 The game started twenty-five minutes ago.
2 Andy was late because he was playing a computer game.
3 Liverpool didn't score first.
4 Liverpool is winning.
5 Paula doesn't think that Liverpool will win.

4 ● 3.09 **Listen to the dialogue. Then practice the dialogue with a partner.**

Paula What's the score?
Andy It's 2–1 for Barcelona.
Paula Who scored first?
Andy Lyon scored after twenty-four minutes.
Paula Really?
Andy Then Barcelona scored after forty-three minutes and again after fifty-six minutes. I'm sure Barcelona will win.
Paula I don't think so. I think it'll be a draw.

5 **ACTIVATE** Change the words in blue in exercise 4 using the *Latest scores* information. Then practice your new dialogue with your partner.

LATEST SCORES		
Chelsea	1–3	Porto
Goals: 4		22, 34, 79 (minutes)
Lyon	1–2	Stuttgart
Goals: 24		43, 56 (minutes)
Internazionale	1–1	Dynamo Kiev
Goals: 42		64 (minutes)
Hamburg	2–2	Arsenal
Goals: 3, 52		19, 44 (minutes)

EXTRA LISTENING AND SPEAKING ◼ Calling a medical helpline

I can get help for a medical problem by phone.

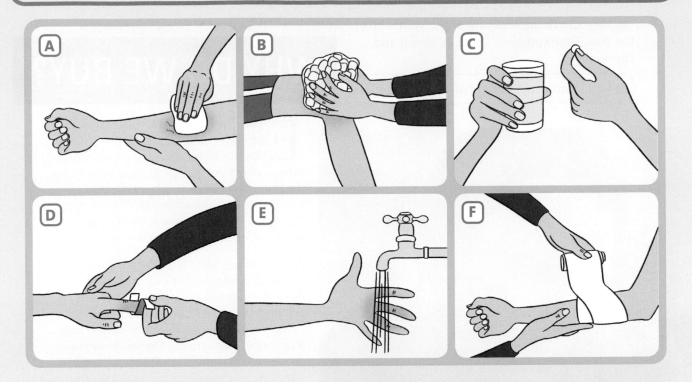

1 Match instructions 1–6 with pictures A–F.

1 Put some ice on it.
2 Put it under cold water.
3 Clean it.
4 Put a bandage on it.
5 Put a Band-Aid on it.
6 Take an aspirin.

2 🔘 3.17 Listen to two telephone calls to a medical helpline. Which instructions from exercise 1 do you hear?

3 🔘 3.17 Study the key phrases. Then listen to the telephone calls again and answer the questions.

> **KEY PHRASES ◯ Calling a medical helpline**
>
> Can I get your name, please?
> How can I help you?
> I burned / bruised / cut my ….
> You need to ….
> You shouldn't ….
> Thanks for your help.

1 What has Lisa done?
2 How did she do it?
3 How does her hand feel now?
4 What has Robert's mom done?
5 What is her plan for tonight?
6 What shouldn't she do?

4 🔘 3.18 Listen and write the sentences. Then listen and repeat.

5 🔘 3.19 Listen to the dialogue. Then practice the dialogue with a partner.

Operator	Medical Direct. Can I get your name, please?
Riley	Yes, it's Riley Mason.
Operator	OK, Riley, how can I help you?
Riley	Well, I've cut my finger and I'm not sure what to do.
Operator	First, put your finger under cold water.
Riley	OK, and then what?
Operator	Then put a Band-Aid on your finger.
Riley	OK, I'll do that. Thanks for your help.
Operator	You're welcome. Bye.

6 **ACTIVATE** Change the words in blue in exercise 5 using your own ideas and the instructions in exercise 1. Then practice your new dialogue with your partner.

Reach Out Options

CURRICULUM EXTRA ● Technology: Advertising
I can understand a text about advertising.

1

1 1.14 Check the meaning of the words in the box. Then complete the text. Listen and check.

> brand   company   essential   non-essential

TOMMY ■ HILFIGER

WHY DO WE BUY?

Every day, people buy products from stores, supermarkets, or the Internet. Some products are essential, but others aren't. An ¹___ product is something that we need, for example, basic food. A ²___ product is something that we want, but isn't always necessary, like clothes with designer labels or a new cell phone.

Advertising is very important for non-essential products. For example, these days, most people have a cell phone. A cell phone company uses advertising to make people change their phone and buy a new one. Advertising also makes people choose a particular ³___. When people buy a new pair of sneakers, for example, they often choose a brand. It's very important for a ⁴___ to make its brand popular with advertising.

Look at the advertisement for Tommy Hilfiger glasses. The people look attractive and cool. But is it the ad, the product, or the brand which is attractive? A lot of people buy the product because they like the brand, even if there are similar, cheaper glasses!

2 Read the text again and write *true* or *false*. Correct the false sentences.

1 An essential product is something that we need to buy.
2 It isn't necessary to advertise a non-essential product.
3 It isn't important for companies to have a popular brand.
4 People sometimes buy products because they like the brand.

3 Look at the two pictures and answer the questions.

1 What products are these advertisements for?
2 Do you know any famous brands for these products? What are they?
3 Are the products essential?
4 Do you want to buy these products? Why / Why not?
5 What other famous ads do you know?

4 ACTIVATE Find pictures of three ads and write short descriptions of them.

Sony Ericsson

DAS NEUE T630
MIT BRILLANTEM FARBDISPLAY UND *QuickShare.*

CURRICULUM EXTRA ● Language and literature: Poetry
I can understand metaphors in a poem.

1 Read the poem and answer the questions.

1 How many verses are there?
2 Does each line have the same number of syllables?
3 Do the words at the end of each line rhyme?

2 🔊 1.29 Listen and read the poem again. Where does the writer live: in a house, a castle, or a school?

My home is a house,
but it is so much more.

My home is a school,
where I can learn and grow.

My home is a city,
full of noise and light.

My home is a café,
sweet and warm.

My home is a castle,
safe from attack.

My home is a forest,
where no one can see me.

My home is a mountain,
it will be there forever.

3 Read the lines from the poem below. Then write *true* or *false*.

My home is a forest,
where no one can see me.

1 The author lives in a forest.
2 The author has trees in his / her home.
3 The author can be alone in his / her home.
4 This extract is a fact.
5 This extract is a metaphor.

4 Find five other metaphors in the poem. Which of them are true for your home?

5 **ACTIVATE** Think of some metaphors about life. Use the ideas in the box or your own ideas. Then write your own poem.

a road   a forest   a tunnel   a party
a journey   a class   a river   an ocean

Life
Life is a journey,
Every day is a new place.

Reach Out Options

CURRICULUM EXTRA ■ **Language and literature: Folk stories**
I can retell a story from another character's viewpoint.

3

The bird AND THE ELEPHANT

One day a colorful bird saw a young elephant. There weren't any other elephants around, and the elephant was lonely and upset. Suddenly, the bird knew what the problem was. The elephant was lost. The bird flew high into the sky and looked for the other elephants. The bird saw them near a river and went back to the young elephant. "Come with me!" the bird said. The bird flew in front and the elephant followed. Finally, the elephant joined the others near the river and the bird left.

Twenty years later, the elephant was in a different part of the jungle and saw a man with a bird in his net. The bird was old, but it was still beautiful and colorful. Suddenly, the elephant recognized the bird. The elephant ran towards the man and made a loud noise. The man dropped the net in surprise and the bird was free. "Why did you help me?" the bird asked. "Because I never forget my friends," said the elephant.

1 🔊 1.42 Look at pictures A–D and put them in the correct order. Then listen, read, and check your answers.

2 Read the story again and answer the questions.
  1 Why was the elephant upset?
  2 How did the bird help the elephant?
  3 Why did the elephant help the bird?
  4 Folk stories often have a moral. Choose the best moral for this story.
    a Help someone and they'll help you.
    b Animals always help each other.
    c Birds have good memories.

3 Complete the information with *first person* and *third person*.

Most stories have a first person narrator or a third person narrator.

A ¹___ narrator is one of the characters, and participates in the story.

A ²___ narrator tells the story, but doesn't participate in it.

4 **ACTIVATE** Imagine that you are the bird in the story. Rewrite the first paragraph of the story as a first person narrator.

One day I saw a young elephant. There weren't …

Reach Out Options

CURRICULUM EXTRA ■ **Natural science: Geological formations**
I can write about a geographical feature.

4

The courses of
A RIVER

1 Check the meaning of the words in the box. Then match them with 1–6 in the diagram. Read the text and check your answers.

> mouth   valley   estuary   meander
> source   waterfall

2 ⊙ 2.13 **Read and listen to the text. Then answer the questions.**

1 In which course does the water travel fastest?
2 What causes erosion?
3 How is the water different in the lower course, near the mouth of the river?
4 Where is the mouth of the river?

3 Match the words in blue in the text with definitions 1–4.

1 a long way from one side to the other
2 with no hills
3 more vertical than horizontal
4 large stones

The source of a river is often in the mountains. The river starts here and the water travels very fast through a steep valley. It carries big rocks and this causes erosion. There are often waterfalls in the upper course of a river.

In the middle course, the water still carries rocks and other material, but they are smaller than in the upper course. The water also travels more slowly. The valley is less steep, and erosion forms curves in the river, called meanders.

In the lower course, the river travels across flat land towards the coast. Near the coast, the river becomes very wide, and the water becomes salty. This is called an estuary. Finally, the water travels into the ocean at the river mouth.

4 **ACTIVATE** Find out about a river in your country and describe it using the words in exercises 1 and 3.

The river is called … .
The source is … .
The water travels … .

CURRICULUM EXTRA ■ Natural science: Adapting to the environment

I can talk about an animal that migrates.

5

ANIMAL MIGRATION

Animals adapt to their environment in different ways. Some change their appearance, for example Arctic foxes, which become white in the winter. Others, such as cobras, produce substances like venom, to help them feed. However, some animals adapt in a different way – they travel thousands of miles to a different habitat. This is called migration. Animals migrate for different reasons. Some, such as salmon, travel from the ocean to rivers to breed, because it's safer for their young there. Others, such as monarch butterflies, migrate south to spend the winter in a warmer habitat. Migration is one of the most amazing phenomena in the animal kingdom.

1 ● 2.26 **Read and listen to the text. Then match the words in blue with definitions 1–5.**

1 produce young animals
2 place where an animal lives
3 move to another place to live
4 eat
5 change

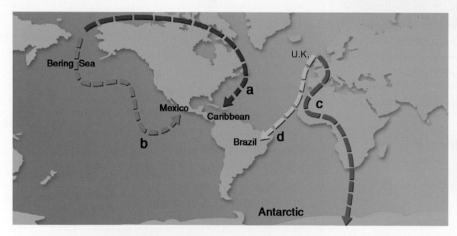

gray whale

Arctic tern

2 ● 2.27 **Look at the map. Then listen and choose the correct migration route for the gray whale and the Arctic tern.**

3 ● 2.27 **Listen again and complete the table.**

Animal	Migrates from	Migrates to	Distance	Time of journey
Gray whale	[1]___	Pacific Ocean, Mexico	9,000 kilometers	[2]___ months
Arctic tern	Shetland	[3]___	[4]___ kilometers	2–3 months

4 **ACTIVATE** **Work in pairs. Find out about an animal that migrates. Complete the table in exercise 3 for your animal. Then compare your animal with another group's animal.**

CURRICULUM EXTRA ■ **Math: Statistics and charts**

6

I can understand different ways of presenting statistics.

1 Check the meaning of the words in the box and match them with A–E in the charts.

> bar chart   y-axis   x-axis   data
> pie chart

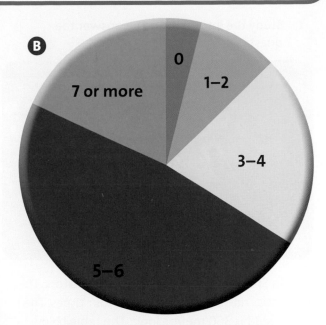

B

0

1–2

7 or more

3–4

5–6

Number of candy bars / week

Healthy eating

SURVEY

We did a survey about healthy eating in my school. We asked all the students how many candy bars and pieces of fruit they eat each week. We recorded the data in different charts. These are the results.

A

Candy bars / week	Number of students
0	32
1–2	72
3–4	168
5–6	384
7 or more	144

Pieces of fruit / week	Number of students
0	38

C

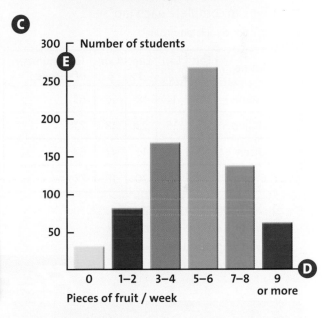

300 — Number of students

E

250

200

150

100

50

0   1–2   3–4   5–6   7–8   9 or more

D

Pieces of fruit / week

2 Study the report and charts. Then write *true* or *false*. Correct the false sentences.

1 There are 900 students in the school.
2 More than 150 students eat 3–4 pieces of fruit each week.
3 Nobody eats nine or more pieces of fruit each week.
4 More than half of the students in the school eat 5–6 pieces of fruit each week.
5 More students eat 3–4 candy bars a week than 1–2 candy bars.
6 Most students don't eat any candy bars.

3 Draw a bar chart for the data below.

Portions of fast food / month	Number of students
0	0
1–2	45
3–4	360
5–6	275
7 or more	120

4 **ACTIVATE** Write true and false sentences about your chart. Then test your partner.

Reach Out Options

CURRICULUM EXTRA ◼ Math: Average speed
I can understand and calculate average speeds.

7

1 Study the information and answer the questions.

In Speedway, there are four competitors. They must ride around the circuit four times. The circuit is 300 meters long. The table below shows the time in seconds that it took four riders to complete each lap*.

*lap = one completed circuit

Name	Lap 1	Lap 2	Lap 3	Lap 4	Total number of seconds
Adams	15	14	18	16	63
Gollob	16	16	23	18	73
Olsen	19	15	13	17	64
Crump	19	21	20	18	78

1 Who had the fastest lap?
2 Who had the slowest lap?
3 Who finished first?
4 Who finished last?

2 Check the meaning of the words in the box. Then read the information and answer the questions.

distance   time   average speed
calculate   equation

To calculate average speed, you need the following equation:
$$\frac{distance}{time} = \text{average speed}$$

Example
Distance: a lap was 300 meters long.
  4 x 300 meters = 1,200 meters
Time: Adams completed the 1,200 meters in 63 seconds

So, average speed: $\frac{1,200}{63}$ = 19.05 meters per second (m/s)

To calculate average speed in kilometers per hour, use this equation:
Average speed in meters per second (m/s) x 3.6 = average speed in kilometers per hour (km/h)

1 Look again at the table in exercise 1. Calculate the average speed of Gollob, Olsen, and Crump, in m/s.
2 Now calculate the average speed of all the riders in km/h.

3 ACTIVATE Read the sentences and find the average speed in km/h for each athlete.

Record breakers!

1 In 2003 Paula Radcliffe completed the London Marathon in 2 hours, 15 minutes, 25 seconds (2.26 hours). The marathon was 42.19 kilometers.

2 At the 2012 Summer Olympic Games, female track cyclists Guo Shuang and Gong Jinjie from China rode 500 meters in 32.422 seconds.

3 In 2009 Usain Bolt ran 100 meters in 9.58 seconds.

4 In his career as a swimmer, Michael Phelps won 22 Olympic medals. In one race he swam 200 meters in 1 minute, 43 seconds (103 seconds).

CURRICULUM EXTRA ■ Language and literature: Stories

I can understand description, narration, and dialogue in an extract from a classic novel.

1 Check the meaning of the words in the box. Then look at the picture and predict which words will appear in the text.

> wolves   bears   castle   houseboat   howling   roar   coach   train   taxi

2 🔊 3.20 Read and listen to the text. Check your answers to exercise 1.

3 Read the information. Then match 1–3 with extracts a–c.

1 Description: what you can see, hear, or feel
2 Narration: what happens
3 Dialogue: what people say

a I arrived at a little town called Bistritz.
b "Where are you going?" they asked me.
c There were mountains, trees, and rivers everywhere.

4 Answer the questions.

1 What type of story is *Dracula*?
2 Do you know the story?
3 What is your favorite type of book?
4 Who is your favorite author?
5 Do you read books in English?

5 **ACTIVATE** Find some more examples of description, narration, and dialogue in the text.

Dracula

Chapter 1

And so, on 4th May I arrived at a little town called Bistritz. Transylvania was a strange and beautiful place. There were mountains, trees, and rivers everywhere. And somewhere high in the mountains was the Count's home, Castle Dracula. I had six hours to wait before the coach came to take me there, so I went into a little hotel. Inside the hotel it was warm and friendly. The people there were all laughing and talking.

"Where are you going?" they asked me.

"To Castle Dracula," I replied.

Suddenly the room was silent and everyone turned to look at me. I could not understand why they all looked afraid.

"Don't go there," someone said.

"But I have to," I answered. "It's business."

They began to talk again, but they were no longer laughing. The coach arrived, and we traveled up into the mountains. Higher and higher it went, faster and faster. The sun was bright, but above the trees there was snow on the mountain tops. Then suddenly the sun went behind the mountains and everywhere was dark. In the forest around us, the wolves were howling. It was a terrible sound.

Suddenly, the coach stopped. A small carriage came down the narrow road on the right. Four black horses were pulling it, and the driver was dressed in black, with a black hat pulled down over his face.

"Where's the Englishman?" he called. "I've come from Castle Dracula!"

He looked strange, standing there in the moonlight, and suddenly I was afraid. But it was too late. I could not go back now.

Bram Stoker

CULTURE ■ Allowance
I can talk about how I spend my money.

1 🔵 1.15 Check the meaning of the words in blue in the sentences. Then read and listen to the text. Write *true* or *false*. Correct the false sentences.

1 All of the people get an allowance.
2 Peter has a part-time job.
3 Peter delivers newspapers.
4 Angela gets $7 an hour for babysitting.

YOU AND YOUR
M$NEY

Do you love spending money? Where does your money come from? Is it an allowance from parents or from a part-time job? How much money do you get and what do you spend it on?

SOPHIE	13

My parents give me $25 every month. It isn't much because I need $15 a month for my cell phone. I usually spend the rest on food and trips to the movies. I don't have a part-time job, but I help at home. I always wash my dad's car on the weekend. That's an extra $10 a week.

PETER	15

My brother and I don't get an allowance, but we have part-time jobs. He delivers newspapers every morning and I work in a café on Saturday afternoons. I prefer doing that because I hate getting up early! I spend all my money on computer games. My mom buys them on the Internet for me because they're cheaper.

ANGELA	14

I get $20 allowance every week. I get extra money when I babysit for the neighbors. They give me $8 an hour. I usually spend $7 a week on magazines or some makeup. I save the rest of the money. I always buy birthday presents for my family with it. I don't need any money for clothes because I go shopping with my mom and she buys them.

2 Read the text again and answer the questions.

1 What does Sophie always spend $15 a month on?
2 How does Sophie get extra money every month?
3 Why doesn't Peter deliver newspapers?
4 Where does Peter buy his computer games? Why?
5 What does Angela spend her money on?
6 Does Angela buy her own clothes? Why / Why not?

3 **YOUR CULTURE** Work in pairs. Ask and answer the questions.

1 Do you get an allowance?
2 What do you usually spend it on?
3 Where do you usually go shopping?
4 Do teenagers in your country often have part-time jobs? What do they do?

4 **TASK** Work in small groups. Do a survey about money. Complete the chart for your group.

NAME	Maria			
MUSIC	$5–10			
MOVIES				
CLOTHES				
CELL PHONE				
FOOD AND DRINKS				
OTHER				

How much do you spend every month on music?

I spend between $5 and $10.

1 🔘 1.30 Read and listen to the text. Where do Ruby and Henry meet their friends?

Ruby
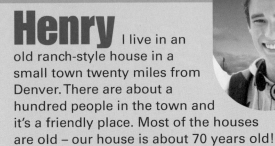

I live on the tenth floor of an apartment building near downtown Denver, in the state of Colorado. I'm looking out of the window in my bedroom right now. I can see lots of streets and houses, but I can also see the mountains about fifteen miles away.

There's a busy street near my apartment building, so it's pretty noisy. Hundreds of people live in the apartment building, but not many people know each other! There's a big shopping mall and a movie theater nearby. I usually meet my friends there after school.

Henry

I live in an old ranch-style house in a small town twenty miles from Denver. There are about a hundred people in the town and it's a friendly place. Most of the houses are old – our house is about 70 years old!

I don't mind living in my town, but I'm sometimes bored on the weekend. There isn't much for teenagers to do here, but they're building some public tennis courts right now, which is great! If I want to go shopping or meet my friends, I can get a bus to Denver. It's thirty minutes from here.

2 Read the text again and answer the questions.

1 Why can Ruby see a lot of things from her bedroom?
2 Is it easy for Ruby to go shopping? Why?
3 Do you think the apartment building is a friendly place? Why / Why not?
4 What is good about Henry's town?
5 How does Henry sometimes feel on the weekend? Why?
6 Is Henry happy about the new tennis courts?

3 YOUR CULTURE Work in pairs. Ask and answer the questions.

1 Is it noisy where you live? Why / Why not?
2 Where do teenagers usually meet where you live?
3 How old is your home?
4 Would you prefer to live in an apartment building or a house? Why?

4 TASK Prepare a class debate on the statement: *It is better living in the city than the country.* Follow instructions 1–5.

1 Divide the class into two groups of people who agree or disagree with the debate statement. You need the same number of people in each group.
2 In groups, write a list of reasons to support your opinion.
3 Take turns to present your reasons.
4 Ask questions after each presentation.
5 Vote for which group presented the best argument.

CULTURE ■ Teenage years

I can describe my parents' and grandparents' teenage years.

1 ● 1.43 Read and listen to the text.
When were Jackie and Lucinda teenagers?

HAPPYDAYS

Amy I live in Golden, Colorado in the U.S. My mom and grandma grew up here, too, but their teenage years were very different.

Jackie There are two things I remember clearly about the 1970s. I was eleven in 1975 and I had a new type of electronic game called Pong. It was like table tennis and we played it on our color television. It was fun! The other thing I remember is the first *Star Wars* movie in 1977. It was at the movie theater for months because it was so popular. I went to see it three times! I also loved disco music in the 70s. I had cassettes of my favorite singers and listened to them in my bedroom.

Lucinda I was a teenager in the 1950s and for me it was a really exciting time. The thing I remember most is the music. There was a new type of music, rock and roll, and a young singer called Elvis Presley became "the king of rock and roll." We didn't have CDs then, so we listened to him on the radio. My parents didn't like rock and roll. They thought it was too loud and fast. I remember some radio stations banned it. I left school in 1961, got married, and became a housewife. Most women stayed at home in those days.

2 Read the text again and answer the questions.

1 Where did Amy's mom and her grandma live as children?
2 Did Jackie like the *Star Wars* movie? How do you know?
3 How did Jackie listen to music in the 70s?
4 Who was Elvis Presley?
5 How did Lucinda listen to music in the 50s?

3 YOUR CULTURE Work in pairs. Ask and answer the questions.

1 When were your parents teenagers?
2 What do you think life was like in your country at that time?
3 What type of music and entertainment were popular?
4 Do you think it's better to be a teenager now? Why / Why not?

4 TASK Write an article about your parents' and grandparents' teenage years.
Follow instructions 1–5.

1 Prepare a list of questions to ask your parents and grandparents about their lives as teenagers.
2 Ask your parents and grandparents your questions.
3 Write a paragraph for each person that you interview.
4 Find some pictures that relate to your text from magazines or the Internet. Stick the pictures on your article.
5 Put your articles on the wall of your classroom and vote for the most interesting article.

I can talk about an adventure sport.

1 ⦿ 2.14 Read and listen to the text. Find the names of the adventure sports in the pictures.

QUEENSTOWN

Adventure capital of the world?

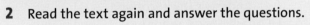

1

New Zealand attracts lovers of nature and fans of dangerous sports. Many of them combine these interests when they visit Queenstown – "the adventure capital of the world." But is Queenstown only for daredevils?

The region has beautiful scenery and a dry climate, so it's ideal for outdoor activities. The first Europeans came to the area in the 1860s to farm and to look for gold. Queenstown was very quiet for 100 years. Slowly, it became a popular fishing and hiking center. Today, adventure tourism is Queenstown's biggest industry.

In the summer, you can choose from bungee jumping, hang gliding, jet boating, mountain biking, paragliding, skydiving, and white water rafting. In the winter, thousands go skiing in the Remarkables, the mountains around Queenstown.

Rachael Turnbull, 73, moved to Queenstown in 1967. "I was living and working in England, but I wasn't happy. There were too many people and there was too much noise. Everything was expensive. Even the traffic scared me while I was riding my bike to work. That's why I came here. It's really peaceful. I love the clean air, the fresh vegetables from my garden, and the sunset on the Remarkables. Thousands of tourists come here for the adventure sports, of course. I don't mind them, but I think there's more to Queenstown than bungee jumping! It's a beautiful place to live."

2

2 Read the text again and answer the questions.

1 What is the weather like in Queenstown?
2 What did the first European visitors do?
3 What activities can you do in the summer?
4 Why do people visit Queenstown in the winter?
5 Why didn't Rachael Turnbull like England?
6 Why does Rachael Turnbull like Queenstown?

3 YOUR CULTURE Work in pairs. Ask and answer the questions.

1 What is the climate like in your country?
2 Which adventure sports are popular in your country?
3 Is your city popular with tourists? Why / Why not?
4 Do you want to try adventure sports one day? Which ones?

4 TASK Make an advertisement for an adventure sport. Follow instructions 1–4.

1 Think about a place where you can do adventure sports, and make notes.
  a Where is the place? (It can be anywhere in the world.)
  b What is the adventure sport?
  c Why is it fun?
  d What is the climate like?
  e What can you say about the area's geography?

2 Make a poster. Write a few sentences about the adventure sport. Add pictures and a map of the area.

3 Put your poster on the wall. Tell the class about your adventure sport.

4 Vote. Whose poster is the most popular?

CULTURE ● National festivals

I can talk about a festival in an English-speaking country.

1 ● 2.28 Read and listen to the text. What do Australians celebrate on Australia Day?

AUSTRALIA DAY

Australia Day is on January 26 every year. It's a national holiday in Australia and it's the country's most important date. The day celebrates the greatest things in Australian culture – the history, the land, the people, and their most important achievements. It's also an opportunity for people to think about the future of Australia.

People organize thousands of fantastic events all over the country. January is the hottest month in Australia, so lots of events are outside. In Sydney, the biggest city in Australia, the day starts at 5:30 a.m. with a barbecue breakfast. Then there is a traditional ceremony of Aboriginal singing and dancing. In the afternoon, there are boat races, concerts, fairs, and special sports competitions.

About half of Australia's population of twenty-two million people goes to an event. The other half celebrates the day at home or on the beach, with family and friends. They have barbecues and they watch the *Australian of the Year Award* on television. Any Australian can win this award. Recent winners include cricket and tennis players, singers, scientists, and politicians. There is also a *Young Australian of the Year Award* for people aged 16–25.

The day ends with fireworks. There are hundreds of huge firework displays all over the country. The biggest display is in Perth, Western Australia. Almost half a million people watch the firework display from the side of the Swan River.

2 Read the text again and answer the questions.

1 What happens in the morning in Sydney on Australia Day?
2 What happens in the afternoon?
3 How do people usually celebrate Australia Day?
4 Who gets the *Australian of the Year Award*?
5 What is the maximum age for the *Young Australian of the Year Award*?
6 Where is the largest firework display on Australia Day?

3 YOUR CULTURE Work in pairs. Ask and answer the questions.

1 What is the most important day of the year in your country?
2 What happens on this day?
3 What do you usually do on this day?
4 Are there any special awards in your country on this day?

4 TASK Find out about a festival in another English-speaking country. Use the ideas in the box or your own ideas. Follow instructions 1–4.

St. Andrew's Day (Scotland)
Canada Day (Canada)
St. Patrick's Day (Ireland)
Thanksgiving (U.S.)
Waitangi Day (New Zealand)
Bonfire Night (England)

1 Complete the table.

Country	
Name of festival	
When?	
Why?	
What happens?	

2 Write an article about the festival.
3 Find pictures and add them to your article.
4 Put the articles on the wall of your classroom. Vote for the most interesting articles.

CULTURE ■ The U.S. in numbers

I can talk about a South American country.

6

1 ● 2.40 **Complete the text with the numbers in the box. Read, listen and check your answers.**

115   3   50   8   3,365   56

THE U.S.: FACTS AND FIGURES

The U.S. is an enormous country, more than ¹___ times the size of Argentina. There are ²___ states and six different time zones across the country. Its longest road, U.S. Route 20, starts in Boston, Massachusetts, on the east coast and finishes in Newport, Oregon, on the west coast, only a mile from the Pacific Ocean. That's ³___ miles (5,415 kilometers) in total!

The U.S. is a land of extremes. It's both one of the hottest and coldest places in the world – with temperatures from ⁴___ °C in California to –64°C in Alaska. It's also one of the wettest and driest places in the world – parts of Hawaii have 12,000 millimeters of rain a year, compared to only 67 millimeters a year in the Mojave Desert, Arizona! You can see the tallest

trees in the world in the redwood forests in California – up to ⁵___ meters tall!

The U.S. has a population of about 313 million, and it's the third largest country in the world. About eighty percent of the population lives in towns and cities, and more than ⁶___ million people live in New York City, the country's largest city. More than ten percent of people in the U.S. speak Spanish as their first language, and that number is growing. Experts think that in the middle of this century, the population of the U.S. will be about 420 million!

2 **Read the text again and answer the questions.**

1 Which is bigger, the U.S. or Argentina?
2 How long is U.S. Route 20?
3 What are the wettest and driesl places in the U.S.?
4 What's special about the trees in the redwood forests?
5 How many countries are bigger than the U.S.?
6 Do all Americans speak English as their first language? Explain your answer.

3 **YOUR CULTURE** **Work in pairs. Ask and answer the questions.**

1 How many regions are there in your country?
2 What's the longest road in your country?
3 What are the hottest and coldest places in your country?
4 What is the population of the largest city in your country?
5 What language(s) do people in your country speak?

4 **TASK** **Find out about a country in South America and complete the table. Then design a tourist information poster and present your information to the class.**

Country	
Size	
Geographical location	
Typical weather	
Population	
Languages	
The future	

CULTURE ■ National sports

I can write about my favorite sport.

7

1 ● 3.10 **Look at the pictures and answer the questions. Read, listen, and check your answers.**

1 What are the sports in the pictures?
2 Which countries did they start in?

Ball games

It's summer and a stadium in the U.S. is full of 40,000 excited fans. Suddenly, everyone stands up and sings the American national anthem. The game between the New York Yankees and the Boston Red Sox is going to start soon. The game? Baseball, of course!

Modern baseball originated in the U.S., and the sport is an important part of American life. Traditionally, people go to a game with all their family. It's very relaxed, sociable, and noisy, and supporters eat, drink, and sing during the game.

The Yankees and the Red Sox are professional teams. There are also professional baseball leagues in Asia and Latin America. It's an Olympic sport, too.

In England, a few thousand supporters are sitting in the rain. There aren't any players on the pitch. They'll continue the game if it stops raining. If it doesn't stop, neither team will win or lose – it'll be a draw. What's the sport? Cricket!

Although England is the home of cricket, the places where cricket is most popular are hot and sunny – Australia, South Africa, South Asia, and the Caribbean. A cricket game lasts for a long time – sometimes five days – and each day there are breaks for lunch and dinner! However, now there is a new, faster version of cricket called Twenty20. There's pop music and the atmosphere at the ground is more exciting. Some people think that Twenty20 will replace traditional cricket some day.

2 **Read the text again and answer the questions.**

1 How do you think the baseball fans feel about the U.S.?
2 What do baseball supporters do while they're watching a game?
3 What happens if it rains during a cricket game?
4 Where is cricket most popular?
5 How long are some cricket games?
6 How are traditional cricket and Twenty20 different?

3 **YOUR CULTURE Work in pairs. Ask and answer the questions.**

1 Which team sports are the most popular in your country?
2 Where did they originate?
3 Do the supporters sing the national anthem?
4 What do supporters usually do when they're watching them?
5 In your opinion, which teams will win championships this year?

4 **TASK Find out about a sport that you like. Use the notes to help you. Then write a fifty-word text about the sport.**

• the origin of the sport
• the countries where people play it today
• the people who play it
• the people who watch it
• a few facts about the sport
• the sport's future

CULTURE ■ The police

I can talk about my dream job.

1 3.21 **Check the meaning of the words in the box. Then complete the text with the words. Read, listen and check your answers.**

bulletproof vest   emergency call   gun   missing person   police officer   police station

A dream job?

I'm Michelle Clark and I'm 28. I joined the police five years ago. I love adventure and helping people, and I've dreamed of being a ¹___ since I was about six. I'm so happy my dream has come true!

One in six police officers in Canada is a woman. It wasn't easy to join, but I prepared a lot. I took a test and a fitness test, I had an interview, and then I got the job!

First, I trained for eighteen weeks at the police academy. Then I started work at my local ²___. I remember my first day clearly. I was working with an experienced officer when we responded to an ³___. I was wearing a ⁴___ over my uniform, and I was carrying a ⁵___. Police officers in the U.K. don't usually carry guns, but they do in the U.S. and Canada. I felt nervous, but really excited as we drove across town to investigate a robbery.

I've done so many different things as a police officer. I've looked for a ⁶___, I've been to car accidents, I've worked at international soccer games, and I've also helped to reduce crime in the local community. Being a police officer has changed my life. It isn't everyone's dream job. I don't work nine to five, I'm often outside in all types of weather, and I'm sometimes in difficult and dangerous situations, but I love it.

2 **Read the text again and answer the questions.**

1 What was Michelle's childhood dream?
2 How did Michelle get her first job as a police officer?
3 What did Michelle do on her first day as a police officer?
4 Does Michelle carry a gun?
5 Has she ever worked at a big sports event? Explain your answer.
6 Does Michelle usually work in a police station? Explain your answer.

3 **YOUR CULTURE Work in pairs. Ask and answer the questions.**

1 What number do you call in an emergency?
2 Have you, your friends, or family ever called the police? Why? When?
3 What uniform do the police wear in your country?
4 Do the police wear bulletproof vests or carry guns?
5 Are you interested in joining the police? Why? / Why not?

4 **TASK Make a presentation about your dream job. Follow instructions 1–3.**

1 Find out about your dream job. Use the Internet or, if possible, interview somebody who does this job.
2 Make notes:
   a What preparation and tests will you need?
   b Where can you do this job? What employers are there?
   c What training are you going to need after you get the job?
   d What will be the best and worst things about this job?
   e Why is this your dream job?
3 Organize your notes and prepare to speak to the class for three minutes. Illustrate your presentation with pictures from websites.

VOCABULARY PUZZLES ■ Everyday objects • Free-time activities

1

1 What does Matthew have in his bag?
Use the code to write the words.

A	B	C	D	E	F	G	H	I	J	K	L	M
▲	✳	♣	◖	■	✚	☆	♠	★	◎	🐛	▮	✳
N	O	P	Q	R	S	T	U	V	W	X	Y	Z
♥	●	♣	◯	♣	✚	◆	►	▼	◎	◆	❖	❞

▲ ◆ ★ 🐛 ■ ◆   a ticket

2 Look at the pictures and complete the puzzle. What's the hidden word?

The hidden word is: ___.

3 Unscramble the letters with the same color. Then complete the sentences.

s	e	e	s	t
e	w	c	e	r	n
a	a	d	a	c	a
e	s	n	v	l	y
r	p	s	e	c	t
d	o	r	s	k	l

Jack	spends	a lot of time playing soccer.
My friends	1	money to buy new clothes.
Ben and Amy	2	an ID card at school.
Harriet	3	a lot of jewelry.
I	4	pictures of my friends.
Toby	5	old concert ticket stubs.
Do you	6	your cell phone in your pocket?

VOCABULARY PUZZLES ● At home • Housework

2

1 Find five more differences in picture B. Write five sentences.

In picture B ...
There's a laptop on the sofa.

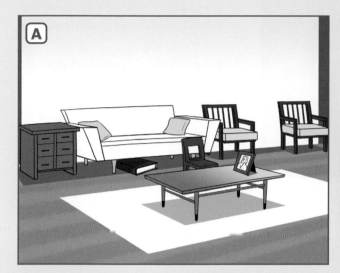

2 Complete the puzzle with words for furniture and rooms.

3 Find the missing letters from the alphabets. Use them to make words and complete the sentences.

CUXM	BLXO	BIJGV	AUVB	MCZS
NFIJS	JYZS	FUHX	FIJKY	FVQJR
LZDO	PUEQ	MTOQ	MZGH	LNDIP
VBGP	RTVC	RDWS	RQCXT	UXGH
WYRHQ	1 WFHD	2 ZPYK	3 WNLP	4 YWBO

Can you **take** the dog for a walk, please?

1 Is Alison ___ her bed?

2 Please ___ the floor now.

3 My brother never ___ the dishes!

4 Can you ___ out the trash, please?

VOCABULARY PUZZLES ● Adjectives: feelings and events • Milestones ③

1 Complete the puzzle with adjectives. What is the hidden word?

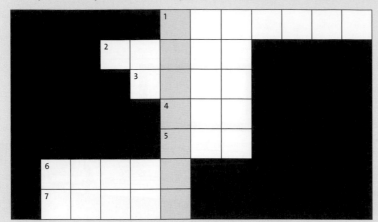

1 On my first day at school I was ___.
2 I saw a ___ movie last night.
3 My cousin is six months old and he's very ___.
4 I want to ___ a job next year.
5 She ___ her first child in 1990.
6 If someone is sad or unhappy, they are ___.
7 If good things happen to you for no reason, you are ___.

The hidden word is: ___.

2 Find ten more life events in the puzzle. Use two or three squares for each one.

buy a house

buy	take	get	a	married
test	be	have	school	~~a house~~
a professional	get	win	go	become
born	leave	child	grow	a
up	to	a competition	a job	home

3 Order the blocks of letters to complete Sam's ambition.

| G R | O V E | A N T | A N | A | T Y . | D | M |

| A T E | I | W | T O | C I | T O | B I G | A D U |

| I | | W | | | | | | | | | | | | | |

| | | | | | | | | | | | | | | | | |

VOCABULARY PUZZLES ● Prepositions: movement • Geographical features 4

1   Agent X works for the secret service but his name is a mystery. Write what he was doing yesterday at different times. Then look at the red letters and write his name.

	s	w	i	m	m	i	n	g	across a lake at 6 a.m.
He was	1								around an island in a boat at 8:30 a.m.
	2								up a high mountain at 11:00 a.m.
	3								through a snowy valley at 3:30 p.m.
	4								off a horse in an accident at 7:00 p.m.
	5								over ten buses on a motorcycle at 11:00 p.m.

Agent X's name is: **W**_____

2   Find and order the words for geographical features.

ocean

1 smuntiano

2 eas

3 trofes

4 alfsl

5 yllvea

6 kale

7 sedtre

8 verri

nacoe

3   Use the letters to make eight more words for geographical features. Use each letter once.

a̶ a a a	c	s s s
e̶ e e e e e	o o	t t
l l l l l	n	i
k	r r r	v

sea

1 r _ _ e _
2 d _ _ e _ _
3 f _ _ e _ _
4 l _ _ _
5 o _ _ a _
6 p _ _ _ _
7 v _ _ _ _ y
8 f _ _ _ _

VOCABULARY PUZZLES ■ Skills and people • Adjectives: qualities ⑤

1 Use the code to write the words. Then choose the correct word to complete the sentences.

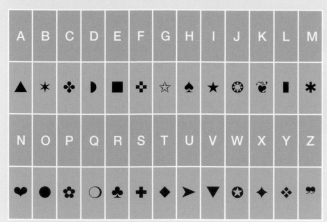

paints

1
2
3
4
5
6
7

Leo **paints** pictures of animals.

a My cousin knows how to ___ a computer.
b I was the ___ of a photography competition.
c John wants to be a tennis ___.
d Leah is a great ___. She makes fantastic food!
e Tom ___ beautiful music.
f Do you ___ children's books?
g Maria is a flamenco ___.

2 Order the letters to make words.
Then fit them into the crossword.

1 y a l p
2 n e c a d
3 p e s o c r o m
4 t w e r r i
5 k o c o
6 t r e n i p a
7 n w i
8 g r e s i n

3 Use the letters to make eight more adjectives.
Use each letter once.

f	u u	t l l	g	a a a a
i i i i i	d d d	r r r	s s s	e e e e
t t t t	m m	o o o	n	c c c

wild

1 p _ _ c _ _ _ _ _
2 r _ _ e
3 f _ _ _ _
4 p _ _ _ t _ _ a _
5 s _ _ p _ _
6 d _ _ _ s _ _ _ a _ e _
7 c _ _ m _ _
8 a _ g _ e _ _ _ v _

VOCABULARY PUZZLES ■ Time and numbers • Adjectives: characteristics 6

1 Complete the puzzle with time and number words.

Across
2 A thousand years is a long time!
3 When there are only two things.
5 Twelve eggs.
7 Wednesday is my favorite ___.
8 The 1990s was an important ___.

Down
1 He's very rich. He doesn't have a million dollars. He has a ___!
2 The ___ of February sometimes has 29 days.
3 I want to live for a ___ and celebrate my 100th birthday.
4 The fastest runners can travel 10 meters in one ___.
6 Another word for nothing.

²M I L L E N N I U M

2 Find seven more time and number words. Then put them in the correct list, from the smallest to the biggest.

F	Y	A	S	R	T	G	W	O	U
G	E	R	W	M	I	I	E	Y	H
H	A	L	F	L	H	S	E	R	U
E	R	E	T	E	O	Y	K	D	N
I	S	T	H	O	U	S	A	N	D
U	E	T	R	P	R	O	Q	H	R
G	D	M	I	N	U	T	E	M	E
T	C	E	H	E	D	R	A	O	D
Q	U	A	R	T	E	R	T	T	R
E	R	B	N	U	S	E	O	N	D

Time	Number
minute	

3 Complete the puzzle with personality adjectives.

P A T I E N T
O
²S
I
T
I
V
E

Complete the opposites of the adjectives in the puzzle.

impatient
1 e _ _ _ _ _ _ _ _ _
2 o _ _ _ _ _ _ _ _
3 u _ _ _ _ _ _ _ _ _ _
4 a _ _ _ _ _ _ _
5 u _ _ _ _ _ _ _ _ _
6 p _ _ _ _ _ _ _
7 s _ _ _ _ _ _

1 Find nine more people in sports. Use two or three squares for each word.

ow	~~cham~~	rep	cap
sup	fi	ref	coa
nal	~~pion~~	ch	er
tain	ee	ager	sor
spon	er	ist	ner
man	ort	port	er

champion

2 Find eight more nouns. Then read the sentences. Match the nouns to complete the sentences with compound nouns.

B	T	J	S	K	I	C	R	G	S	A	R
A	R	J	B	S	B	K	A	U	O	S	T
S	W	I	M	M	I	N	G	L	C	D	O
K	Q	C	F	A	T	T	P	D	C	O	U
E	C	M	A	I	E	E	Y	S	E	E	R
T	E	N	N	I	S	P	F	E	R	T	N
B	N	P	Y	D	F	M	V	A	L	K	A
A	T	E	N	N	I	S	C	S	L	G	M
L	G	C	F	U	B	O	W	O	H	R	E
L	C	H	A	M	P	I	O	N	X	A	N
A	L	G	C	R	R	M	B	T	W	C	T
U	I	N	S	T	R	U	C	T	O	R	D

I'm crazy about basketball. I'm a **basketball fan**.
1 Michael Phelps is a ___ ___.
2 The ___ ___ is about ten months long.
3 Serena Williams won more ___ ___s than her sister Venus last year.
4 I teach people to ski. I'm a ___ ___.

3 Use the letters to complete the labels for the pictures. Use each letter once.

~~aaaaa~~	c	d	~~eeee~~	g	i	l
~~mmm~~	p	rr	s	~~tt~~	u	y

track and field **team**
1 tennis ___
2 rugby ___
3 bike ___
4 table tennis ___

VOCABULARY PUZZLES ● Feelings • Injuries

1 Order the letters of the same color to make adjectives to match the prepositions.

R	I	E	R	U	O	N	D	S	T
I	N	T	C	H	O	A	E	F	G
E	F	B	N	O	S	R	O	S	T
G	R	I	H	D	A	I	E	D	I
E	T	E	D	D	T	D	E	N	W

bad at
1 ___ about
2 ___ at
3 ___ of
4 ___ in
5 ___ about
6 ___ of

2 Use the letters to make five injury verbs. Use each letter once.

a	k	eee	ii	nn
p	s	tt	rrrr	uu

bu r n
1 c _ _
2 b _ _ a _

3 b _ u _ _ _ _
4 b _ _ _
5 s _ _ _ i _

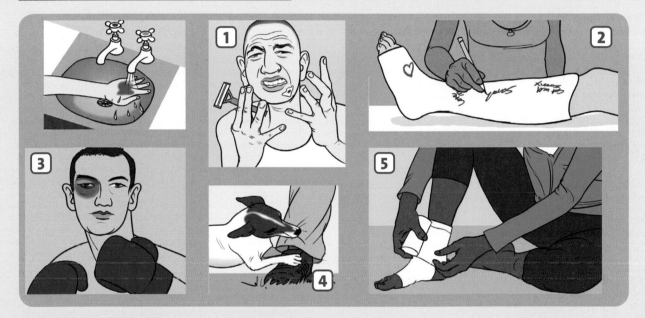

3 Jodie has had an accident at a tennis match.
Order the blocks of letters to find out what has happened.

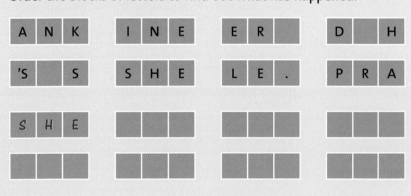

A N K		I N E		E R		D	H

' S	S		S H E		L E	.		P R A

S H E								

OXFORD
UNIVERSITY PRESS

Great Clarendon Street, Oxford, OX2 6DP, United Kingdom

Oxford University Press is a department of the University of Oxford.
It furthers the University's objective of excellence in research, scholarship,
and education by publishing worldwide. Oxford is a registered trade
mark of Oxford University Press in the UK and in certain other countries

ISBN: 978 0 19 485316 3

Printed in China

This book is printed on paper from certified and well-managed sources

ACKNOWLEDGMENTS

The publisher would like to thank the following for permission to reproduce
photographs and video footage: Alamy Images; Amnesty; CERN; Corbis; Getty
Images; Google; MK2; NASA; Photolibrary; POST; Rex Features; The United
Nations; The Wellcome Trust; Zooid.

*The authors and publisher are grateful to those who have given permission to reproduce
the following extract of copyright material:* p.103 extract from *Oxford Bookworms 2:
Dracula* by Bram Stoker retold by Diane Mowat © Oxford University Press 2008.
Reproduced by permission.

*The publisher and authors would like to thank the following teachers for their
contribution to the development of this course:* Romaine Ançay, Ursula Bader,
Dominique Baillifard, Kinga Belley, Jaantje Bodt, Michel Bonvin, Coralie
Clerc, Teresita Curbelo, Yvona Doležalová, Lukas Drbout, Pierre Filliez,
Olga Forstová, Christelle Fraix, Attie van Grieken, Roger Grünblatt, Çağrı
Güngörmüş, Christoph Handschin, Joe Hediger, Jana Vacková Hezinová,
Maria Higina, Jaroslava Jůzková Martin Kadlec, Urs Kalberer, Lena Kigouk,
Joy Kocher, Murat Kotan, Marcela Kovářová, Jitka Kremínová, Lucie
Macháčková, Doubravka Matulová, Jitka Melounková, Dana Mikešová,
Noémi Nikolics, Sabrina Ragno, Denis Richon, Sonja Rijkse, Susanna Schwab,
Dagmar Šimková, Jana Šimková, Nuria Smyth, Lenka Špačková, Rita Steiner,
Anne-Marie Studer, Milan Svoboda, Anneli Terre-Blanche Maria Cecilia Verga,
Marta Vergara, Donna Van Wely.

The publisher and authors would like to extend special thanks to Ursula Schaer *for
sharing her insights and for her contribution to the course.*

The publisher and authors would like to thank Sue Sileci *for her valuable work in
developing* Reach Out.

Illustrations by: Mark Draisey p.21, 26, 27, 28 (elephant), 46, 47, 76, 86, 87, 98;
Peter Ellis/Meiklejohn p.78 (black eye), 113, 117, 119; Kevin Jones Associates
p.115; Joanna Kerr p.91; Dave Oakley/Arnos Designs p.112, 118; Andy Parker
p.18 (room), 38 (mountains), 69, 89, 99, 103; Greg Roberts/Sylvie Poggio
p.18 (teen at door), 97; Stephanie Srickland p.78 (bandage), 95.

Commissioned photography by: Chris King pp.14, 34, 44, 54, 84.

Cover photographs: Photolibrary (Rafting/Glow Images, Couple taking
photograph/Photodisc/White, Teen girls doing homework/Andersen Ross/
White); PunchStock (University students on campus/moodboard);

*The publisher would like to thank the following for their permission to reproduce
photographs:* Alamy p.14 (iPhone/ST-images); Alamy Images pp.9 (cinema
tickets/shinypix), 9 (train tickets/mpworks), 9 (ID card/Dinodia Images),
10 (Radius Images), 12 (metal hunting/Angela Hampton Picture Library),
17 (Apple iPhone/Alex Segre), 17 (wallet/D. Hurst), 20 (Vintage Cadillacs/
Transtock Inc.), 23 (Rolls Royce/imagebroker), 28 (Students in class/Bubbles
Photolibrary), 29 (Dr Martens boot display/Malcolm Freeman), 40 (Niagara
Falls/Coaster), 42 (lighthouse/Mike Briner), 42 (The Black Forest/tbkmedia.de),
52 (Elephant artist painting/Mark Phillips), 52 (woman & dog/Mark J. Barrett),
53 (blue marlin/WaterFrame), 55 (Tintin books/Niall McDiarmid), 56 (Thai
ridgeback dog/Petra Wegner), 59 (signposts/Gavin Wright), 59 (William
Shakespeare/Pictorial Press Ltd), 64 (Richard G. Bingham II), 68 (Referee/
PhotoEdit), 68 (Captain of football team/Richard Wareham Fotografie),
68 (Exhausted tennis player/Action Plus Sports Images), 77 (Swimmers/
Michael Dwyer), 79 (Climbing/Jim West), 81 (Shy teen boy/Angela Hampton
PictureLibrary), 88 (divers/Louise Murray), 96 (Train interior/David Crausby),
105 (Denver skyline/Jim Havey), 105 (Ranch/EditorialByDarrellYoung)'

107 (Queenstown, New Zealand/David Wall), 107 (speed boat/Robert
Harding Picture Library Ltd); Alex Maguire p.30 (Artist Stephen Wiltshire);
BNPS Pix p.52 (Octopus playing with Rubik's cube/Phil Yeomana); Corbis
pp.5 (Amanaimages), 28 (girl with money/Jose Luis Pelaez, Inc.), 37 (Baby
in bath tub/H.Armstrong Roberts/ClassicStock), 37 (Rock 'n Roll dancing/
Bettmann), 39 (Christ statue in Rio/Reuters), 39 (Walking over hot coals/
Sukree Sukplang/Reuters), 44 (Diving/Jean-Yves Ruszniewski/TempSport),
45 (surfing dog/Vince Streano), 49 (*Portrait of young Mozart*/The Gallery
Collection), 49 (Leona Lewis), 59 (Clock in Grand Central Station/Alan
Copson), 59 (Marathon runners/Richard H. Cohen), 62 (Johnny Depp/Toru
Hanai/Reuters), 67 (woman with papers/John Lund/Marc Romanelli/Blend
Images), 79 (Fried Scorpions and Noodles/Owen Franklin), 82 (Venomologist/
Mick Tsikas/Reuters), 108 (Aboriginal dancers/Will Burgess/Reuters); Fotolia
pp.11 (Camel caravan/Dmytro Korolov), 42 (Death Vallye/Matthew Carroll),
59 (100 celebration cupcake/Danny Hooks); Getty Images pp.6 (Two students
in lab/Sean Justice/Photonica), 10 (Novice Buddhist monk/Hugh Sitton/
Photographer's Choice), 16 (Hip hop musical group/Blend Images/Jon
Feingersh), 17 (The Twilight Saga dvds), 28 (father & son/Jamie Grill/Iconica),
28 (boy in cinema/Erik Dreyer/Stone), 28 (Dog/John Dolan/The Image Bank),
29 (Lightning/Valentin Casarsa), 29 (schoolgirl/Peter Dazeley/The Image
Bank), 33 (Elizabeth Blackwell/Time Life Pictures), 35 (Wedding couple/
Jupiter Images), 35 (Old lady having fun/Lyndsay Russell), 36 (Playing tennis/
Lori Adamski Peek/The Image Bank), 37 (1950's family watching television/
SuperStock), 37 (A bride and groom/Lambert/Hulton Archive), 37 (Group
on the beach/Terry Husebye/The Image Bank), 40 (Blondin's Feat/General
Photographic Agency), 41 (Alain Robert/New Straits Times/AFP), 42 (The
South Pole/Sue Flood), 42 (The Rocky Mountains/Michael Melford),43 (skier/
Peter Cade/Iconica), 49 (*Portrait of the Bronte Sisters*, c.1834/PatrickBranwell
Bronte), 51 (Skateboarder Danny Way/2005 Getty Images), 55 (Imagno/
Austrian Archives), 57 (LadyGaga's shoes/AFP), 57 (Lady Gaga), 59 (Calculator/
Jupiter Images), 62 (JenniferAniston/WireImage), 67 (guitarist/Michael
Sharkey/Stone), 67 (businessman/Thomas Barwick/Stone), 68 (Football
supporter/AFP), 68 (Reporter interviewAmerican football player), 68 (British
formula one driver Jenson Button/AFP), 71 (Formula One car/Paul Gilham),
72 (Paralympics Sitski event/AFP), 72 (Disabled women's basketball
team), 79 (Rollercoaster),79 (Lightning storm/Lyle Leduc), 79 (Cockroach/
AFP), 79 (Teenager talking to students/Keith Brofsky/Uppercut Images),
82 (Volcanologist/Mario Cipollini), 82 (Farmer in harvesting machine/Fuse),
82 (Trawlerman), 88 (Karate/Jupiterimages), 93 (man on phone/John Lund/Marc
Romanelli/Blend Images), 108 (Fireworks over Sydney/Romilly Lockyer/The
Image Bank); iStockphoto pp.6 (computer classroom/Lisa Klumpp), 9 (mobile
phone/dem10), 9 (wallet/Kenneth C. Zirkel), 9 (jeans/largeformat4x5),
9 (orange t-shirt/sumnersgraphicsinc), 9 (mp3 player/yuriyza), 9 (key/
redmal), 9 (backpack/Darren Mower), 14 (hat/Darlene Sanguenza), 14 (watch/
ronen), 14 (door key/pidjoe), 17 (Keys/Mark Bolton), 28 (baby/Aldo Murillo),
28 (crying/Corby Chapin), 29 (laptop/T Cstin), 41 (Skydiver/Jeff McDonald),
41 (Motorbike stunt/Marc Summers), 41 (Ski jumping/Ben Blankenburg),
41 (Heart in the sky/Nicholas Campbell), 56 (dog/Madjuszka), 56 (Saint
Bernard/Dennis Mesias), 59 (Remote control close up/mbbirdy), 60 (Elevator
panel/Alex Gumerov), 63 (star signs/Cihan Demirok), 108 (family barbecue/
Catherine Yeulet); John Fowler p.111 (Policeman/contact Photographers
Direct); Nature Picture Library p.29 (bear catching salmon/Eric Baccega); NB
Pictures p.49 (Chandra Sekhar); Oxford University Press pp.9 (coins/Brand X
Pictures), 12 (coins/Brand X Pictures), 15 (Teen girl/Digital Vision), 22 (Teen
in bedroom/Blend Images), 28 (lSmiling girl/Creatas/Comstock), 61 (Earth/
Collection Mix: Subjects), 65 (planets/Corel), 67 (artist/moodboard), 67 (chef/
Digital Vision), 67 (singer/moodboard), 74 (Brand X Pictures), 77 (Boys with
skateboards/Photodisc), 88 (drama/Thinkstock), 90 (girl/Design Pics), 90 (young
girl/Comstock), 90 (School boy/Chris King), 90 (Portrait of teen boy/Digital
Vision); Photolibrary pp.14 (skateboard/Corbis), 29 (looking under bed/Adriana
Williams/Cusp), 50 (Young scientist/Corbis), 77 (Gymnasts/Peter Muller/
Cultura); Press Association Images pp.49 (Judit Polgar playing chess/BAS
CZERWINSKI/AP), 72 (PA WIRE); PRShots.com pp.14 (Bag/M&S), 14 (Jumper/
M&S); PunchStock pp.29 (The White House/National Geographic); Rex Features
pp.20 (Britney Spears home/Most Wanted), 31 (Barack Obama), 32 (Bill
Gates/Sipa Press), 32 (Serena Williams/Action Press), 49 (Michael Phelps/
Olycom SPA), 57 (Lady Gaga/Brian J. Ritchie/Hotsauce), 83 (Stunt woman/
Mike Forster/Daily Mail); Ripley's Entertainment Inc. p.13 (Joshua Mueller
and his collection of Converse trainers/From Ripley's Believe it or Not 2008);
Sarah Kavanagh p.70 (Sarah Kavanagh, Irish motor racing driver); Science
Photo Library p.19 (family/Peter Menzel); Shutterstock pp.17 (Skateboarder),
25 (Modern flat/rodho), 42 (Sahara Desert); Tony Mihok p.111 (Policewoman).

*Although every effort has been made to trace and contact copyright holders before
publication, this has not been possible in some cases. We apologise for any apparent
infringement of copyright and, if notified, the publisher will be pleased to rectify any
errors or omissions at the earliest possible opportunity.*